Dressage
by the
LETTER

Dressage by the LETTER

A GUIDE FOR THE NOVICE

Moira C. Harris

Photography by
Sharon P. Fibelkorn

HOWELL BOOK HOUSE
New York

For the Harris family:

Steve, Charlie, Max, and Rex

Howell Book House
A Simon & Schuster Macmillan Company
1633 Broadway
New York, NY 10019

MACMILLAN is a registered trademark of Macmillan, Inc.

Library of Congress Cataloging-in-Publication Data

Harris, Moira C.
    Dressage by the letter : a guide for the novice / Moira
C. Harris : photography by Sharon P. Fibelkorn.
        p.   cm.
    Includes index.
    ISBN 0-87605-726-1
    1. Dressage.   I. Title
SF309.5.H28   1997
798.2'3—dc21   96-29681
                                                           CIP

Manufactured in the United States of America

10 9 8 7 6 5 4 3 2

Contents

Acknowledgments

I thank the following for their assistance in preparing this book:

First and foremost, Lynn Ann McQueeney, of LAM Dressage, Lake Forest, California, who has provided guidance throughout this project with her technical knowledge and has been unwavering in her encouragement; Lesley R. Ward for her excellent editorial support and her brilliant sense of humor; Susan Hoffman Peacock and Bradoon, Ltd.; the riders and horses of Serrano Creek Ranch Equestrian Center, Lake Forest, California, including Karen Cribbs and April Success; Susan Ennis and Heineken; Pamela Hampton and Harley; Susie Bretting, Brette Steele, Lindsay and Patty Patterson; Audrey Pavia and Rosie; Nancy Mooney and Jazzy; Guy Garrett and Windy T.B. Laskowski for their help at El Toro Tack and Feed; HST; Joel Reavis; Gerald for 100 Ways; Tolcat, a Nightingale; Ronayr; and to family and friends who were put on hold while I labored at my Macintosh.

Dressage— An Overview

Chapter One

*B*eauty. Power. Grace. Teamwork. These words describe dressage, a sport that is often regarded as the epitome of a horse-and-rider partnership. From the most elementary levels of competition to Grand Prix, the highest, dressage reflects years of dedicated training to create harmony between horse and rider.

Two decades ago, a scant handful of enthusiastic, devoted riders were involved in the "groundbreaking" of the sport in the United States. But today the story is entirely different. The United States Dressage Federation, the national governing body, has seen a dramatic upswing in membership and show attendance in the past few years. Dressage is currently the nation's fastest growing equestrian sport. State dressage societies are offering more shows each year, and plenty of opportunities exist for riders new to dressage to try their hand at hundreds of schooling shows all over the country.

Dressage seeks to promote excellence not only from competitors, but also from teachers of the sport. Certified riding instructors must pass stringent tests, based on a universal standard, in order to qualify for USDF approval.

To completely understand what dressage is and how it affects the horse's body, mind, and aptitude, we need to appreciate the dedication and teamwork that make up a successful horse-and-rider pair.

What Is Dressage?

The term *dressage* comes from the French word for "training." Dressage is a way to school and improve a horse, but it is also a competitive sport that many equestrians take part in. Dressage is technical, yet it has artistic merit.

Dressage is more than just flatwork. It's more than the pirouettes and leaps that the Spanish Riding School of Vienna is famous for. The purpose of dressage is to help horses to become supple, attentive, straight, and relaxed and to move forward in balance. It can improve any type of riding, from jumping to reining. The people who excel in dressage want to achieve something more than simply posing on the back of a horse. Their goal is to communicate better and develop harmony with their mounts.

Dressage has a long history. In the fourth century B.C., Xenophon, a Greek, wrote about principles of horsemanship based on gentling horses in their training while they were taught new movements and tasks. In Renaissance times and in succeeding centuries, dressage was the domain of aristocrats and royalty. By the eighteenth century, dressage had become the classical school of riding we know today. European armies employed dressage in training their cavalries. It was as a military event that dressage first became an Olympic sport in 1912. Now, it is an activity that all riders are able to participate in and gain unique insight into the equine/human relationship.

The Grand-Prix tests of today are much more demanding than the original 1912 tests, but the horses that competed in dressage earlier this century also had to complete a jumping test and an obedience test as a three-phase event.

Dressage in the United States

In the 1970s, it could truly be said that the United States was an up-and-coming nation in dressage. It was also during this decade that the United States Dressage Federation was born in the heartland of the country, Lincoln, Nebraska. While membership grew slowly in the first few years, recognizing only thirty-four competitions in 1974, ten years later, the USDF had 17,845 members and recognized 483 competitions. In 1996, the USDF had nearly doubled its membership to 34,127, and the numbers continue to swell.

Many people became aware of dressage because of Hilda Gurney and Keen, the chestnut Thoroughbred she competed with in the 1976 and 1984 Olympics. This pair gave horsemen and -women their first glimpse of a superstar team and helped push dressage to the forefront of equestrian sports.

Because the number of riders involved in the sport is still relatively small, the media give it limited exposure, so dressage will remain obscure outside the equestrian community. It is quite different in Europe, however, where there is major media coverage of equestrian events and great spectator attendance. Europeans often treat their horse-and-rider teams as we do our superstars of football, baseball, and basketball. The United States continues to give its scant equestrian coverage to Thoroughbred racing, instead of the Olympic disciplines.

Interestingly, cable television is beginning to offer more coverage of show jumping and international dressage, so in future years, large corporations may decide to sponsor events and in turn give the sport the recognition it deserves.

Today's Sport

Dressage competition involves a test comprised of patterns and transitions, a marked dressage court, and a horse-and-rider pair. In order for a horse to advance to the next level, he must pass the objectives of his current level. Each level adds something new, building upon the objectives of the previous level.

Dressage competition involves a test comprised of patterns and transitions, a marked dressage court, and a horse-and-rider pair.

The test has a formal air. The rider enters the arena and halts straight down the center line, then salutes the judge. The rider performs the entire test and, at the end, salutes the judge once again.

The most elementary tests, called Introductory Level, are only a couple of minutes long, while a Grand-Prix test—an Olympic-level test—requires that the rider perform complex movements and patterns for almost ten minutes. But no matter what level is ridden, horses riding at the same level are all graded with the same ideal in mind. Riders receive points for each dressage test movement, and the score is added up and averaged out at the end.

The performance of the pair is judged in a test. The performance of the horse and how he is influenced by the rider is scored in every box, while the rider is critiqued at the bottom of the score sheet. The reasoning behind this is that if the rider is flawed, the horse's performance will be also. If the rider is good, the horse will be influenced positively by him or her. Judges do bring to the table the elements that they consider most essential to the ideal ride, but for the most part,

Points of the Test

Horses will receive a score from 1 to 10 for each test movement. The closer the horse and rider come to achieving the goal, or directive, the more points awarded. The points are then tallied, and the final score is averaged by the total possible points.

The horse and rider receive their score both in points and as a percentage (such as 240 points and 65 percent).

the judging in dressage is much more objective than other equitation disciplines.

To the layperson, dressage may be difficult to evaluate. The nuances that separate a good ride from a great ride are subtle and can sometimes be detected by only the seasoned eye. Dressage judges not only grade on the horse's ability to do the movements but they also look for expression, which could be described as "class" or "flash" in another discipline. Even a layperson can appreciate a horse that makes dressage look easy, effortless, and brilliant. Dressage begins with the basics, with the horse accepting transitions at a walk, trot, and canter, while staying on the bit and engaging his hindquarters. Once the horse learns the basic movements, he then begins the more advanced lateral maneuvers, such as shoulder-in, haunches-in, and half pass, and learns how to correctly collect himself and then stretch out in a longer frame. He learns self-carriage—his natural body carriage—but with a rider astride.

The overall benefits of dressage are many. Horses become more ridable when they have had some dressage training. After a horse has been taught classical principles, he begins to have more confidence in himself and moves with more balance and freedom. Many horses become more "tuned in" to the rider and pay better attention. They become more receptive to the rider's aids.

Dressage and You

You undoubtedly have a strong interest in dressage and may want to give it a try with your own horse but don't know how to get started. It can be overwhelming to take on a sport that seems so entrenched in formality, protocol, and tradition, but the reality is that dressage is a very contemporary sport that people from any riding background can enjoy.

Because America is such a big country, many people who live in remote areas have to learn to ride by themselves. They may get the wrong idea about dressage by just observing. For instance, they may try to imitate what they think is a dressage horse on the bit, by pulling the horse's nose in instead of pushing the horse forward into the bridle with leg and seat aids. By trying to imitate without understanding, they are doing both themselves and their horses a disservice.

Some people do not have the benefit of riding with a trainer. They may only be able to take a clinic once a month and therefore may "get lost" within that month and often start from scratch at the next clinic. But despite any disadvantages you may have, you can get started by first obtaining as much background information on dressage as you can, and then getting the correct assistance you need to succeed. Whether you're a pleasure rider who has logged in miles on the trail or a show rider who has spent time in the ring focusing on equitation, you can still make the transition into dressage.

Adding dressage to your current riding program can help your horse psychologically as well as physically. Not only can it refresh a tired routine, making your horse happier with the variety, but it also works different sets of muscles, aiding in his flexibility and overall athleticism.

It also helps you as a rider in very much the same way, allowing you to develop muscles and tone in different areas and providing you with a different way to balance yourself in the saddle. Dressage can help you develop a secure seat and a better feel for your horse. It can help your mental outlook as well, giving you new challenges to work toward.

Dressage can give you an opportunity where there may not have been one before. For instance, if your horse has had limited success in western pleasure classes because he did not have the proper headset, he can go on to an exciting new career. If he doesn't get pinned in hunter classes because he isn't quite fancy enough over fences, he still has a terrific chance of being competitive in the dressage arena.

Dressage for Hunter/Jumper Riders

Most hunter or jumper trainers will strongly agree that dressage helps make horses more supple, attentive, energetic, and responsive, yet they may not emphasize it as part of their regular lesson programs. So much time is spent teaching the correct position over fences and riding technical courses that often there is little time for working on the flat in great detail. Many hunter/jumper riders are concerned about their horse's ability over fences, and they overlook the most important element in a hunter or jumper round: the flatwork. However, for really successful hunt-seat riders, the jump is merely another stride. They realize that the trip is determined by the way they ride their horse on the flat.

Some hunter or jumper trainers encourage their students to take up elementary dressage to learn how to rebalance their horses after a fence, how to supple them for smooth turns, how to move them laterally for better corners in the arena, and how to keep the ride going forward with a steady rhythm. Dressage for the hunter or jumper makes the horse a better athlete and aids the rider in improving the lines of communication.

Most successful hunt-seat riders realize that their success over fences is determined by the way they ride their horse on the flat.

Dressage also helps direct the horse around his course more effectively. We've all seen rough riders hauling their horses around a course of fences by the face. This type of poor steering encourages a sloppy jumping style, running out, stopping, "chipping in," diving, and worse. A horse will perform better, achieve proper striding, and use the arena effectively if his hunter or jumper rider uses elements of dressage to keep him straight, in front of the leg, and accepting the contact of the bit. A ride will appear more relaxed and smooth if the rider moves the horse over with her legs and seat instead of her hands.

Taking up dressage does not necessarily mean you have to "switch over" to dressage and shun what you've been doing all these years—unless you have the desire to. Dressage will enhance your current riding program. Its various exercises and routines help your horse to become strong and flexible, and he will perform better in his current field.

Dressage for Western Riders

The winning western pleasure horse carries himself in a consistent frame. While the speed of the western pleasure horse's gait is entirely different from what is striven for in dressage, the horse must still be light and responsive to the aids. He must be guided easily and move with balance and ease while performing the required gaits. The rider possesses a balanced seat that doesn't interfere with the horse. Western pleasure riding and dressage share some of the same objectives: moving with power and being propelled from the hindquarters while being relaxed, supple, collected, and responsive.

Both the western pleasure horse and the dressage horse must be light and responsive to the aids.

If you want to school your western horse in dressage, you may find that he will respond more easily to neck reining. You will sharpen up your horse's responsiveness to being moved over from the shoulder and not the face. A horse that is trained in dressage is attentive and responsive, and generally doesn't have the problems associated with sourness, such as tail wringing and high head carriage—things that you don't want to see in a pleasure horse.

The western sport that bears the most resemblance to dressage is reining. With its patterns and movements, it teaches a similar style of competitive thinking. Anyone who has watched freestyle reining can easily see the similarities to a freestyle dressage routine. For riders who want true quality gaits (no shuffling trots or four-beat lopes), dressage teaches horses how to use their bodies effectively.

Dressage for Gaited Breeds

Some of the loveliest dressage horses come from the ranks of saddleseat riding, where they formerly had careers as country pleasure horses. Their training stresses responsiveness, which results in horses that are sensitive and move off of the rider's leg. Their forward, animated way of going, coupled with their natural knee motion and active stride, make horses such as Arabians, Saddlebreds, National Show Horses, and Morgans a good choice for switching over to dressage.

The best thing about dressage is that it is, for the most part, an equal opportunity sport. While both the hunter ring and the western pleasure show pen suffer from a bit of breed bias, dressage does not. Riders and horses are scored according to a set ideal, and competitions are open to all breeds, sizes, and colors of horses and ponies. A horse will receive the same marks whether he is an Appaloosa, Connemara, Arabian, or Thoroughbred.

Is Dressage for You?

Above all, you should determine the level at which you want to participate. Dressage involves a lot of arena work, so if that bores you, you may end up being quite unhappy. If your horse must have his head set for his primary sport, such as western pleasure, then you must seriously consider how a dressage horse carries himself and ask yourself if you want to undo the horse's current head carriage.

You will have to have an open mind, because riding dressage is different from how you currently ride, even if you ride hunt-seat. It takes time to develop a good dressage horse, so you must have the patience for the demanding work. Establishing the basics with your horse is critical, so you must be comfortable with the repetition required in the sport. For those with the determination to succeed, dressage does wonders for the rider, instilling self-confidence and reinforcing mental discipline.

While you shouldn't have to give up your present career in riding, you may find that dressage becomes all-consuming, and you may choose to concentrate primarily on it. If you do still enjoy jumping, you may want to expand your repertoire and consider combined training (eventing), which includes dressage and jumping. One goal of dressage is to create the ultimate equine athlete, and there are few better ways than combined training to show how versatile your horse has become. If you are interested in eventing, contact the United States Combined Training Association (USCTA) at P. O. Box 2247, Leesburg, Virginia 22075.

Riders who want to prepare their horses for the show ring must spend many months and years developing their horses gradually and completely. Anyone who wants "instant results" will have to look for a sport other than dressage. However, for those who want to build a relationship, block by block, with their horse, the rewards are many. Dressage riders consider their horses to be their partners, and not just a means to an end. Most will also tell you that above all, they never stop learning. If dressage sounds good enough to be your sole passion, then get ready for fun, hard work, and satisfaction.

What to Expect

As with any new sport, it's hard to know what you'll be getting into until you immerse yourself in it. The number of enthusiasts varies by region, but since dressage is growing so rapidly, you'll no doubt find a strong contingency fairly close by where you live.

Realistic goals for the person new to dressage depend on time, money, and determination. Talent is also a factor but only a small part of the picture. No matter what period of your life in which you decide to take up dressage, your age will not be a hindrance in competition or schooling at any level.

Much of your success will depend on how competitive you are. Do you want to show your horse occasionally just for fun, or are you looking at serious competition? At the local show level, even an average horse can do a nice job in the arena. It doesn't need to be a perfect sporthorse.

Yet competition is only one aspect of the sport. You don't ever have to show if competing is not your primary goal. Even without the element of showing, dressage is still beneficial to every horse and rider. As long as your body is supple enough to take the motion of the horse, you can ride dressage—even into your retirement years!

You don't have to be born with a "good seat," although it doesn't hurt to be a naturally good rider. Being able to develop a good "feel" for your horse is more important. Many riders who don't have the perfect body associated with riding—the long legs or the svelte figure—can be quite talented in dressage. With patience and determination, plus a strong love for the horse, any equestrian can be successful.

Success also comes from hard work during lessons. Dressage is an intense discipline. There is a right way to do things, and most instructors will show you the correct tools that will turn you from passenger to rider. Once you get involved in a lesson program and find other enthusiastic riders, you can expect to find camaraderie like no other, which can also aid in your learning process.

Dressage competitions differ from other horse shows in a number of ways. In dressage, you ride a test of required movements in the arena, alone. Judges score you numerically, on a point system, and you are given written comments to help you see where you need to improve and where you did well. At schooling shows and entry-level shows, judges may even ask you to come forward after the test and discuss elements of your ride. This is very different from most horse shows, where riders are often left to wonder why they didn't get pinned. And this time, since you are the only person in the ring, you won't get "lost in the crowd."

Another difference in shows is that you are assigned a time to ride your test. Consequently, you can time your arrival to the show grounds so you don't have to wait around endlessly for your turn. Also, set times allow competitors to get mentally prepared and warm up their horses efficiently without overworking them.

Don't expect that the judges at shows will be more forgiving because you are just starting out. Judges judge on what is correct. They cannot ignore the basics that all horses and riders must observe, even at the lowest of levels. You can expect, however, that judges will make constructive comments on your test that can often be encouraging to the novice rider.

Competitions

There are many different types of dressage competitions, and you can choose the one that will best give you the opportunity to test your knowledge. Whether it is a schooling show or just a local unrated event, you will feel at home with other riders like yourself who are just getting into the sport. Once you are ready to move up to more serious competition, you can attend a recognized, or rated, show. These are usually held by the local or state dressage chapter, and they give you the opportunity to compete for local points and year-end awards.

Showing dressage is a unique experience because the judge gives you extensive written feedback on your ride.

Showing dressage does not hurt your finances any more than showing another discipline. The cost of tack is similar to that of English tack. Horses do not need any special training gadgets. Dressage lessons are not more expensive than other lessons; although, extra money can be spent on the plethora of riding clinics and educational opportunities offered to dressage enthusiasts. Overall, investing in your dressage career is worthwhile, and it can be exciting, too.

Know Your Tests

Dressage tests are designed by the American Horse Shows Association (AHSA) and FEI from the lowest level (Introductory Level) to the highest (Grand Prix). There are four tests per lower level. It's important to get a copy of the tests that you wish to perform so you can understand the purpose of your level, as well as the movements and their "directive ideas," which is what the tests set out to accomplish. The tests are uniform so that your level's four tests are the same, regardless of where they are performed.

You may want to attend one or two shows that you would qualify to enter to see what the event is like from a spectator's point of view. Usually, the entry-level tests are scheduled in the morning, so make it a point to spend a few hours watching the horses and riders who will be your fellow competitors. See what makes a successful ride, and note how riders and horses react to showing. Then you can be better prepared when the time comes for *you* to enter the arena, halt, salute, and be on your way!

The FEI

The Fédération Equestre Internationale (The International Equestrian Federation) is the international governing body for equestrian sports. The term "FEI levels" means the international levels of Prix St. Georges, Intermediate I, Intermediate II, and Grand Prix.

Chapter Two

Your Horse's Suitability

When most people hear the word dressage they think of one thing: WARMBLOODS! The idea that only warmblooded horses excel in dressage comes from the fact that most upper-level mounts are indeed European sporthorses, including the Hanoverian, Trakehner, Oldenburg, Westphalian, and Dutch and Swedish warmbloods. These breeds shine in the sport because Europeans have selectively bred them for dressage for decades. They have the athletic conformation and the ideal gaits, as well as the tractable disposition that makes them perfect for the discipline.

For most riders just starting out, the FEI levels of dressage are something to aim for—far ahead in the future. It may take many years of riding and practice before that happens. If you count yourself among those who are not yet striving for international-caliber competition, your own horse will do just fine at the lower levels. You'll be able to bring out the best in him, while developing better communication and cooperation.

Some purists would argue that if you know how to ride and you have mastered the basics of dressage, you should then move on to a "real" horse: one that is already schooled in dressage. It is true that it is easier to learn on a trained horse—a "schoolmaster"—that has the conformation and the ability to do what you ask while you are learning. However, most people do not have the money to buy an already "made" horse, nor do they want to. While having to learn the sport at the same time as your horse puts you at a slight disadvantage, it is far more rewarding to see the athletic development of your own horse taking shape as a result of your diligent efforts.

Dressage doesn't have the typical breed prejudices of other disciplines. In the dressage show arena, you'll see a variety of breeds, such as this Norwegian Fjord.

The nicest aspect of dressage is that it takes into account each individual horse's natural ability, with the aim of improving the three natural gaits—walk, trot, and canter—and making him a pleasure to ride. Dressage is one sport that can be called an all-breed sport. Go to an A-rated hunter show and you will stand out if you don't have a solid-colored, lanky Thoroughbred-type. Similarly, western shows will shun any animal that doesn't fit the well-muscled Quarter Horse/Paint/Appaloosa mode. Dressage doesn't have the typical breed prejudices that are seen in other disciplines. Moreover, the USDF and many breed associations join together to offer incentive programs and year-end awards for individual breeds.

Many horses can make the transition to dressage. Some have the innate raw talent for it, while others can be brought along if they have the right conformation and temperament. At the lower levels, all horses can compete equally. Not everyone needs to be on a future Grand-Prix horse.

From Introductory Level to Third Level, the gymnastic exercises include figures, movements, and transitions. Dressage training uses these exercises to strengthen and build the horse's muscles, supple and improve his balance, improve his gaits, and make him more responsive. As the horse progresses in his training, the exercises become more difficult.

But does your own horse have what it takes to do dressage? The answer to this question is generally yes. Some are just more suited to excel in the sport than others. Training difficulties can be overcome more quickly than conformational problems, and here's how you can assess your own horse's shortcomings or assets to determine what his future will be in the sport.

As far as breeds go, every breed association will tout its horse as being versatile, and while conformation varies from horse to horse, we can speak in generalities about breed types. Western breeds, such as Quarter Horses, Paints, and Appaloosas, are generally smaller in size than their English-bred counterparts, but all are known for their calm, tractable temperaments and their ability to accept new situations.

Some novice riders can be intimidated by the hotter breeds. These people can turn to a western breed for a steadier mount. Most western breeds that are western pleasure winners, however, are built "downhill," which makes it harder for them to collect and use their hindquarters effectively.

Hotbloods, such as the Arabian and the Thoroughbred, have the intelligence and athleticism to take on the sport of dressage. Both have the ability to learn quickly and possess the endurance and stamina to perform the necessary work. In the past, the Arabian was criticized as a dressage horse because of some Egyptian bloodlines that result in flat-crouped horses. These horses may have difficulty lowering their croups and moving well underneath themselves. The larger Polish Arabians and the Shagya Arabian (a Hungarian strain), however, have the size and conformation suited to the sport.

The American Saddlebred and the Morgan have the lovely action and flash that are assets in the dressage arena. Breeders of Morgans and Saddlebreds have seen that there is a market for their breeds in dressage, so they are beginning to breed horses that are built for it. Saddlebreds that are not too narrow, and "old-style," larger Morgans are enjoying success in the show arena.

Conformation Counts

As noted earlier, the descriptions of the breeds are very general, and exceptions to the rule, both positive and negative, exist. There are Arabians performing at the Grand-Prix level, and there are warmbloods that are only suited to be trail horses. To determine your own horse's suitability, think of the conformational assets and challenges that he has in order to evaluate what kind of dressage career he might have. Different sports have different conformational requirements, which not only enhance athletic performance but also ensure soundness throughout the horse's career.

Every dressage expert has his or her own formula for a good equine dressage candidate, and some expert opinions will conflict with others. But the most important thing to remember is that a good horse is not just made up of one factor. You must look at the whole picture before deciding how well your horse is suited to dressage. In the most basic terms, a horse that has three good gaits, decent conformation, and the ability to use his body effectively will have the makings of a true athlete in the sport.

From the top to the bottom, observe any conformational shortcomings in your horse that can be overlooked and any that might need a second look.

To check if a horse has a good neck, measure the length from his poll to his withers. The measurement should be twice as long as the distance from his throatlatch to where his neck meets his chest. A horse with this type of measurement is able to carry his neck in a more relaxed fashion. A short neck can't bend as well as one that is in balance with the horse's body. A very long-necked horse may have a tendency to overbend or just bend at the neck and not bend the entire body. Such a horse may naturally carry his neck crooked and be resistant to traveling straight. A ewe-necked horse, also known as a horse that is built "upside down," is usually muscled on the underside and does not bend well at the poll. The horse should be thin through the throatlatch and should have a fairly large mouth, as it can be more difficult to fit a bit properly in a very small mouth. Standard bit sizes and widths can

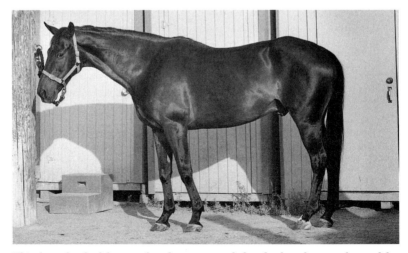

This long-backed horse often has too much bend when he travels, and he has difficulty keeping his body straight.

still cause a horse to develop mouth problems—physical or behavioral—in petite-muzzled horses.

He should have a high enough wither to stabilize the saddle in the right position. The horse's shoulder should have enough slope to absorb concussion and produce a long stride. He should have a nice 45-degree angle to the slope of his shoulder so that his forelegs can move freely with a flowing gait.

A horse with a straight, level back is ideal. A horse with a short back will have trouble bending. On the other hand, a horse with a long back may have trouble stepping underneath himself and may have difficulty keeping straight and "upright" because he tends to bend too much and in every direction! Weak backs are swaybacks (with a dip) or roached backs (with a hump).

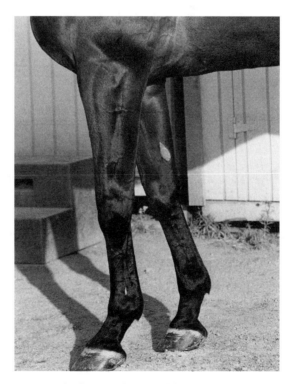

This horse is over at the knees, which could lead to front end problems if he is not warmed up properly or wearing protective legwear.

Your horse's legs and feet are crucial in determining how he moves. The bones should align so that one area does not get stressed more than another. Large hooves with strong hoof walls are the best. Small hooves take more force per square inch than larger hooves and can therefore be prone to lameness. Sloping pasterns not only allow for more freedom of movement for the horse, but they also absorb concussion well and promote better suspension—the time during one stride of a gait in which no hooves touch the ground. Straight pasterns are predisposed to concussion injuries. The dressage horse should have fairly open stifle and hock angles. Sickle hocks or weak hocks are more detrimental than front-end problems, such as calf knees or being over at the knees. But if the horse does have serious front-end problems, such as a crooked knee, he will be susceptible to weakness and strain.

This horse has cow hocks, which are prone to injury and lameness.

The horse should track up when in motion, that is, the horse's hind feet should step into the footprints of the front feet. However, he should not overtrack too much at the beginning of his training, as he will be difficult to collect later. He should step underneath himself at all gaits, but particularly at the canter. A horse that has impulsion uses his engine—his hindquarters—and this energy travels through the back and over the topline to lift his front.

He should have a strong croup that is only slightly sloped. The horse that is built "downhill" is higher at his croup than at his withers. Such a horse has a center of gravity that is farther forward and, consequently, will be heavier on the forehand. "Uphill" horses are naturally higher at the withers, which enables them to lift their front ends more effectively.

A Word on DAP

If you're truly serious about finding out whether your horse has the makings to go far in the sport, you can try a technique that some of the major trainers use to determine a horse's potential. The horse that has movement known as diagonal advanced placement (DAP) will more than likely make an excellent dressage horse.

To determine if your horse possesses DAP, videotape him at the trot. It must be a relaxed trot, and the horse must be carrying his head naturally and trotting on a level surface. Take your tape home and play it back on a frame-by-frame advancement. While you already know that the trot is a two-beat gait and the legs move in diagonal pairs, the horse whose back foot lands before the front one does (just mere milliseconds) has a positive DAP. If the horse's front foot in the diagonal pair lands before the back, experts say that it is not built for big-time dressage. If the feet land at the same time, the horse has limited ability in the sport. In other words, the horse may not work off of his hind end enough or carry himself properly. If you indeed see the hind foot strike before the fore, he has the makings of a dressage star.

The DAP technique is not really essential for those just beginning to get into dressage, and since most dressage riders can happily spend their entire competitive careers in the lower levels, it is not necessary either. But this evaluation can give you better insight into your horse's overall movement.

Making the Best of Your Horse

If your horse has conformational flaws, take heart. He can still manage just fine as long as he travels soundly and doesn't have one fault that compounds another, interferes with him by causing an injury, or causes you to incur extra expenses.

There is more to the sport of dressage than the size and shape of your horse. As long as he is strong, well put together, and has the right mental attitude, you can succeed.

The horse's temperament is indeed a huge consideration. For a person just starting out in dressage, a horse that is kind, easy to handle, and respectful of people is a good prospect. Your horse should complement your riding style. Some riders need a quiet horse they can push, while others do better with a strong horse that goes on his own. A willingness to do what is asked definitely compensates for mild conformational flaws. Your horse should be athletically inclined to do the work of dressage, but if he does not have the temperament for the sport, the talent he was born with will not be brought to the surface.

A horse that enjoys dressage is enthusiastic about work. He is not sour or lazy, but is instead kind and intelligent. In any discipline, the program that you choose for your horse should include plenty of variety. The rider is responsible for not boring her horse with whatever type of riding she chooses, but the horse should also have a decent attention span and not get easily distracted. He should be curious and not fearful of new tasks or new experiences. Additionally, horses that are obedient learn to obey their rider's aids and will find it easy to perform with confidence.

A horse that has the ability to relax has won half the battle in dressage. Overly sensitive horses or green horses often have difficulty relaxing and therefore have problems executing the key elements necessary for dressage's lower levels. Many green riders who make the mistake of getting a green horse may find dressage more difficult than any other discipline.

Videotaping your horse and playing it back in slow motion will give you a good idea of how well your horse carries himself and uses his body without a rider.

When evaluating your own horse, look at some of his previous performances if they are available on videotape. It's a good idea to begin to build your video library so that you will be able to compare his progress at regular intervals. Tape your horse while he is turned out without a rider, too. See the differences in movement as he trots freely. Do you see potential with self-carriage as your horse steps underneath himself? Or does your horse paddle out behind himself, with his neck thrust upward, moving hollowly, never tracking up? Is he heavy on the forehand, never shifting his weight behind? Or does he send himself forward with strong hindquarters?

Some problems will improve with training, while others are indications of poor gaits that can only be made better minimally.

Ride Evaluation

Have a friend videotape you while you are in the saddle so that you can evaluate your horse's performance. See if you can get him to relax at the walk first, and then really ask him to move forward to an extended walk. Check to see if he drags his feet and creates clouds of dust. Do you feel the swing of his walk? Is he leaving a hind hoofprint in the same place as (or in front of) the front foot?

When performing your ride evaluation of your horse, trot him on a loose rein and try to feel how he travels, in balance, with even footfalls, stepping underneath himself.

Put him on a loose rein at the trot and try to feel what he is doing. Does he travel crooked or unbalanced? Do his footfalls match evenly? Is the rhythm marred by tripping or stumbling? Is it so painful to sit his trot that you never can? Finally, ask for his canter. If he has energy at the canter and uses his hind end to propel himself forward, you've got something to work with in the future.

Horses undoubtedly improve with schooling. Good training can change an average horse into a very nice mount. Riders who "work with what they've got" often compensate for their horse's shortcomings by being extra accurate during their tests. They make sure that their tests are correct and that their horse hits all of his transitions at the right spots. They work on making their horses move forward and straight and "through" (round and on the bit). They help their horses to be the best that they can possibly be.

PROFILE #1 April, a fifteen-year-old Quarter Horse mare, was previously a western pleasure horse. She and her former owner successfully competed in regional shows as well as shows sponsored by the American Buckskin Horse Association. Her current owner, Karen Cribbs, started her own riding career when she was in her forties by taking hunt-seat lessons. "While my trainer was showing me Thoroughbreds for sale, a friend told me about April. It was love at first sight."

April Success, a Quarter Horse, formerly worked as a western pleasure mount.

Because April was not built like the lanky hunters she had been looking at, Karen decided that she did not feel the need to jump her. "I'd never even heard of dressage, but when I saw the dressage trainer at my barn riding, I remembered that

(continues)

She is now schooling successfully at Training Level.

April had some dressage training in her youth. I began taking lessons, and I was hooked."

April and Karen currently school at Training Level, and Karen believes that dressage is helping increase the mare's fitness, strength, and confidence. "She has limited suspension in her trot and canter, and she's built downhill," she says. "Sometimes she can be grumpy or lazy. We are working on more impulsion and response to aids. But her attitude is much better. She really seems happy."

PROFILE #2 Phinneas, or Phinney, a seventeen-year-old Appaloosa gelding and a do-it-all kind of horse, had shown at western-pleasure, trail, hunters-over-fences, and breed shows prior to being leased by Lynn McQueeney. "Phinney did really well in dressage, and I think it was mostly due to his incredibly willing attitude. He got scores of 72 and 73 percent at First Level and almost qualified for the year-end championship show."

Phinneas, a versatile Appaloosa gelding, competed in trail, western pleasure, and hunter classes before . . .

Phinney's challenges were his conformational flaws. "He was over at the knees; he had sickle hocks and cow hocks. He was a little on the older side, so toward the end he became more unsound." Lynn said that being a colored horse was also a challenge, so he had to be extra accurate and correct to get good marks. Lynn took him up to Second Level before his age and conformation halted his otherwise successful career.

. . . moving into dressage, where he competed successfully up to Second Level.

PROFILE #3   A nine-year-old registered Standardbred gelding, Heineken's first career began in an unusual way for most horses, on the harness-racing track. When owner Susan Ennis purchased him, she did not know what his potential would be as a dressage horse. While his overall conformation was good, his former training on the racetrack had to be overcome. "I consider him a 'hot' horse," says Susan. "He has a lot of energy and is very sensitive to the leg. We are still dealing with the challenge of him interpreting my leg aids as meaning 'fast' and 'faster.'"

Heineken, a Standardbred, was a former pacer like the one shown above. He had to relearn trotting before he could be taught the basics of dressage.

Heineken has benefited from dressage by becoming more agile and stronger overall, and by learning to carry himself straight. His muscle tone has improved, as has his stamina. Mentally, says Susan, it has also added a new dimension to his personality. "Heinie has always been very fun-loving and playful, but now he has the ability to play bigger!" However, his intelligence and attitude will be key elements in how far he can go beyond his current Training Level schooling.

Heineken now moves in a relaxed manner because of his dressage training.

USDF All-Breed Awards

The USDF was one of the first national show associations to encourage riders and owners of different breeds to compete on a national level. The All-Breeds awards program is designed to recognize successful competitors of different breed categories.

If you compete at USDF–recognized competitions, your scores are recorded during the season to determine the year-end winners. To be eligible, your horse must be registered with your horse's breed organization sponsoring the competition and both you and your horse must belong to the USDF. Hundreds of awards are given out every year, and the program continues to grow, so don't be left out!

Getting Started

Chapter Three

There's so much to do when you are just starting out in any specialty sport, be it dressage, skiing, or cycling. Unless you have endless cash flow and serious vacation time, it is best to prioritize what you'll need to start out and then budget your time and money wisely. While it seems as though you will need a great deal of equipment to begin with, some things can wait, while others you should think about doing right away.

Your Dressage Saddle

To ride dressage, you must be able to sit in a dressage position, and it makes sense to do this in a saddle designed for the sport. In dressage you sit deeper and more upright than in a hunt-seat saddle; consequently, the dressage saddle has a deep, secure seat. When you relax your hips, your legs drop down along the sides of the horse. The longer flaps and the correct knee roll of the dressage saddle facilitate this. While some jumping saddles are called "close contact," the design of the dressage saddle also permits close contact, since all hardware is recessed or repositioned to eliminate any possible interference.

This isn't to say that you won't be able to ride dressage unless you buy a new saddle. Plenty of people school and show in their English saddles, which are perfectly legal in the show ring. But you will be fighting against what the saddle is made for—jumping—unless you own an all-purpose saddle, and even these saddles fit the bill only partway. Western saddles are not recommended for schooling, as they place the rider in an incorrect position and restrict the feel between rider and horse.

Your saddle is the single most important piece of equipment that you will use on your horse. At the very least, an ill-fitting saddle will make a horse uncomfortable and, in most cases, will completely hamper the horse's ability to perform. Poor-fitting saddles give your horse a sore back and may also cause a host of other problems, from subtle lameness to bad behavior. By contrast, a saddle that fits your horse as well as you enhances the athletic performance of you and your horse. The trick is to choose a saddle that first fits you, and once it passes that test, it must fit your horse.

Determine Your Needs

Before going to a tack store, set some limits for yourself, and try your best to stick to them. Determine what your commitment level is, and add this to your maximum budget. If you are just getting started and are only planning to complement your pleasure riding or you're just adding dressage to your repertoire of, say, hunt seat or eventing, then you may want to stick with the most economical selection available. A good rule is to buy the best quality you can afford. However, if you are making dressage your main sport, you would benefit from selecting a higher-quality saddle that will not only break in nicely, but will also last a lifetime and have excellent resale value.

As the sport continues to grow, saddle manufacturers now have more to offer that suits riders' levels of experience and budgets. Because so much is available, the first-time buyer can feel intimidated when all of the saddles seem to look alike

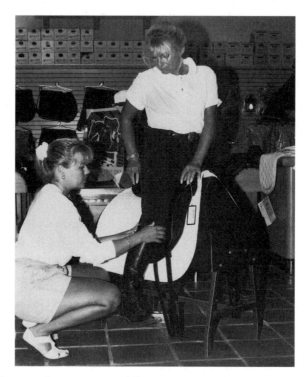

When shopping for your new saddle, go to a store that has a good selection and a knowledgeable sales staff. Wear your boots and breeches if possible, and try to sit in many different models.

in the tack store or catalog. Grades of leather vary, just as workmanship does. At the lowest end of the spectrum, you will find saddle packages for about two hundred dollars that are complete with stirrup leathers, irons, a girth, and a saddle pad. While this is an inexpensive way to get into a dressage saddle, the leather is usually a lower-grade import from India and often has a foul "fish" smell to it. This leather is often weak, stiff, or full of imperfections. The workmanship, including the stitching, tree, and panel stuffing, may not be very high quality either, so you may have trouble reselling this type of saddle later on if you decide to upgrade.

Synthetic saddles have a suede-like or leather-like finish that is often difficult to tell apart from real leather. They clean up with soap and water in minutes and are very durable and inexpensive.

Synthetic saddles present an affordable choice for those who must stick to a strict budget. Synthetics have either a suede-like or leather-like finish, and some top-of-the-line synthetics are often difficult to tell apart from real leather. Because they are made of imitation leather, they have no break-in time. They clean up with simple soap and water in minutes and are very durable. Some saddlers will tell you that one minor drawback to synthetics is that they do not form to your horse's back as a leather saddle would, but most are designed so that they provide an excellent fit anyway.

English, Argentinean, North American, and European saddles make up the remainder of the best saddles. They will vary in the grade of the leather, the deepness of the seat, the build of the tree, the placement of the knee roll, the design of the panels, and the finish of the saddle, but all are built with the similar goal of keeping the rider in the right position for the sport.

Saddle Components

All saddles are built on a tree, which is the saddle's framework. Most trees are made of laminated beech wood, although other woods are used. Sections of the wood are first heated and then pressed into shape. They are then jointed together and covered with webbing. Steel plates are added to reinforce the head and gullet, above and underneath the tree. Some saddles will have trees made of other materials, including polypropylene, fiberglass, nylon, and other plastics. Synthetic saddles usually have trees made of synthetic materials. The stirrup bars, from which the stirrup leather hangs, are riveted to the tree. A dressage saddle pommel is usually fairly straight and upright, and the cantle is fairly high. The seat size is usually measured in inches.

Nearly every saddle is built with a spring tree, meaning that there are two pieces of thin metal attached to each side of the tree to create give. Spring trees extend the life of the saddle and give the horse and rider more comfort. The tree determines how the saddle will fit a horse's back, and it comes in wide, medium, and narrow widths. The dressage saddle's tree is designed with either a normal or a cut-back head, to fit a variety of wither configurations.

You may see advertisements for saddles with an adjustable tree, which can be made to fit a variety of horses or a horse that is hard to fit or changing shape. (As horses go up in levels, their withers, for example, can change shape with the added muscle tone.) Because an adjustable tree is relatively new technology, and many people find it difficult to set the saddle tree correctly, some riders are skeptical about its durability and effectiveness. For other riders, however, it offers one solution to a sometimes challenging situation.

The panels of a saddle have contact with the horse's back. They help distribute the rider's weight evenly across the saddle. Panels are often flocked—or stuffed—with wool, but some models have foam, wool felt, and synthetic stuffing.

The panels will determine how well the saddle (along with the tree) fits your horse. The gullet between the panels should leave the horse's spine free of any contact. The panels should allow for freedom of movement at the horse's shoulders and withers.

Some manufacturers add gel to the seat to absorb concussion and make the saddle more comfortable from the first day you ride in it.

Quality Saddles

You should look for a well-built dressage saddle that has a moderately deep seat and is well balanced from the pommel to the cantle. The deepest part of the seat should be in the center of the saddle, and it should fit you more securely than a western pleasure, English close contact, or even an eventing saddle. When you are sitting properly in the saddle, you should naturally be in the deepest part of the seat. You should be able to maintain your correct body position, with your shoulder, hip, and heel lining up and your weight on your seatbones. Your pubic bone should not hit the pommel. You should easily be able to stay with the horse's center of gravity. The saddle will support you where you need it and give you the means to effectively communicate with your horse. It fits correctly when you hardly know it's there.

Although it may feel comfortable, don't choose a saddle that puts you in a "chair" position, or else you will not be able to use your body effectively. Also, if the seat is too deep, you may find that it's impossible to get out of. A very deep seat does not allow the novice rider to develop a good posting trot. Similarly, a saddle with a really high cantle will keep nudging you forward onto the pommel.

In the dressage saddle, the flaps are placed straight down, underneath the rider's seat, and they are longer than those on hunt-seat saddles. You ride with a longer stirrup, which allows you to wrap your legs around your horse more effectively and provides you with steadier leg contact against the horse; thus, you are in a more vertical position. The position of the stirrup bars is important in dressage, as they need to be set far enough back so that the leg falls underneath the deepest part of the seat. The bar should be horizontally positioned so that when the stirrup leather hangs vertically, you are able to get your heel directly underneath your hip and sink your weight down. If the bars are too far forward, keeping your leg underneath you properly will be an effort.

The knee roll is just in front of the knee and offers support for the entire leg to stay down and under the rider's body instead of slipping forward.

The knee roll is just in front of the knee to offer support to the entire leg so it can stay down and under the rider's body instead of slipping forward. Some saddles have tiny knee rolls, while others have some pretty substantial padding. Choose what makes you secure without restricting your riding. In addition to knee rolls, dressage saddles also have thigh blocks to help keep your leg position secure and increase your leg contact.

You must choose a girth that does not hamper the horse. A girth that is too long can put the buckles in the way of the horse's elbow, causing chafing.

Most saddles today have long billet straps and are cinched up with a short girth. This is so the girth buckles are not in the way of the rider's leg and the flaps can lie smoothly against the horse's side. You must choose a girth that does not get in the horse's way, either. A girth that is too long can put the buckles in the way of the horse's elbow, causing chafing if the horse hits them as he travels.

Dressage saddles differ from hunt-seat saddles in another way. While all saddles measure from the front nail to the middle of the cantle, because of the flat surface of a close-contact saddle, a rider who may fit a 16-inch jumping seat will probably need to buy a dressage saddle that is an inch larger. When shopping, don't just go by size alone. A saddle from one maker may feel different from one by another maker, even though the saddles may be the same size.

Fitting Saddle to Horse

The saddle must fit the horse. It should fit without any extra padding, as the pad is merely there to protect the saddle from sweat. It must be able to distribute your weight evenly on your horse's back so no pressure points cause him discomfort or injury. The pommel should put no pressure on the horse's withers. If your horse has high withers, a saddle with a cut-back head will accommodate them.

A dressage horse may change size across the withers as he goes up the levels. As the horse gets into better condition, his topline changes and muscles develop from his neck, down the withers, and over the croup. The horse may also experience changes due to a different feeding regimen. A normally over-weight animal may get more fit, or a slender horse that is put on a high-calorie diet may muscle up nicely.

Conformation is always a consideration. A slender, narrow horse or a horse that is wasp-waisted (with a wide barrel and a narrow girth) may have difficulty keeping the saddle forward in the correct position without a breastplate. Horses with narrow or flat sternums may have their saddles slide too far forward and may need to have a foregirth. High or long withers can be hard to fit. Your goal should be to choose a saddle with a tree that parallels the withers and touches the sides of the withers evenly with no pressure points.

GOING SHOPPING   Unless you are able to have your saddle custom made, you will have to do some hunting to find the one that is right for both you and your horse. Try not to be swayed by slick advertising or a good salesperson. Don't just buy the first saddle you sit in.

Shop at a store that has a decent selection of saddles and where you feel comfortable browsing. Tell the salesperson what your needs are. Try to sit in a variety of saddles, and if the sales staff can only offer you one or two to sit in, you may have to look elsewhere. If they keep steering you to the model that "everyone rides in" or the "store special," it may be time to check out another store.

Wear your boots and breeches, if possible, and have the salesperson put the saddles on a stand in front of a mirror so that you can check your position and measure the fit. Place the saddle so that the lowest point of the seat is midway between the pommel and the cantle. This way you know you are at least starting off with a balanced seat. Place your hand behind you while seated; there should be about a hand's width of space behind your buttocks. While this measurement can vary, too little space will have you bouncing against the cantle. You will know if the seat is too large because you will be swimming in it.

See that the twist of the saddle, just below the pommel, feels like the correct width for you. The twist will set your comfort level. Usually, a narrower twist will be more comfortable than a wide twist, particularly for women. However, one that is too narrow for your particular build will make you feel as though you are sitting on a saw horse. A twist that you feel comfortable on will cause no problems, but a saddle with too wide a twist will get you in the groin.

The flaps should fit the length of your leg as well, as too long a flap will make it hard for you to feel your horse's sides. With your leg in a dressage position, the flap should end just a few inches below your knee.

An ideal shopping situation would be to trailer your horse down to the tack shop and try the saddle on him there, but since this is hardly feasible for most people, taking the saddle on trial is the next best thing. Purchase your saddle from a store that offers a good trial-and-return policy. Some stores will only allow a two- or three-day trial, while others will give a you a week to thirty days. This does not mean that you can belt around the countryside during this trial period. You are still responsible for the product. If the saddle does not fit on your first ride in it, you should not ride in it again, but should instead return it and either choose another to take on trial or get your money back.

It may take several trials to find a saddle that truly is a good match for you and your horse, but don't get discouraged. Sometimes you *can* find a saddle on the first fitting.

You can purchase a used dressage saddle as well. Used saddles are plentiful, and you can begin looking for one at tack shops that take them on consignment, through ads in newspapers and on bulletin boards in feed shops, and by word-of-mouth. Be careful when you are buying a used saddle. The tree may be twisted, stressed, or broken, and the panels may be irregular or conformed to another horse's body. Depending upon how well the saddle was cared for, you could be looking at a good deal or somebody's "white elephant." There's no guarantee when you buy a used saddle, so be very sure that it fits before handing your money over.

TEST RIDING   When trying on the saddle, first make sure that your horse's back is clean. Then place it directly onto his bare back in a well-lit area. Do not place the saddle too far forward, or it will inhibit your horse's shoulder and his movement. If you were to place it too far back and you were to ride in that position, it would cause your horse pain. Make sure it ends up just behind the shoulder and that it sits perfectly level at the deepest part of the seat (the center of balance), then check the fit.

If the saddle clunks down onto his withers and the gullet hits your horse's spine, the tree is too wide. If the saddle perches above without the panels connecting to the length of his back, looks pinched, or does not appear to be level with the saddle sloping downward, the tree might be too narrow. You should see daylight as you look from the cantle through the gullet to the pommel. Run your hand under the flap to feel for even contact of the saddle's panels, and lift the flap to check for any light coming through. If you do see light, this indicates that the panels are "bridging." Bridging means that the panels are putting pressure on part of the horse's back but

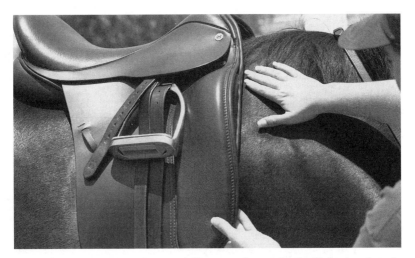

Place the new saddle without a pad on your horse's back. Make sure it ends up just behind the shoulder and sits perfectly level at the deepest part of the seat.

You should see daylight as you look from the cantle through the gullet to the pommel.

are not distributing weight properly because they do not meet the horse's back completely. You should not be able to rock the saddle from side to side.

Check for even pressure underneath the panels.

If you find that the saddle has even pressure underneath and you have ample room at the pommel and cantle (four fingers' width is fine), then it's time to sit in it. It is important to remember that the saddle will feel slightly different now than when you sat in it at the tack shop.

Your next step is to take a clean, thin, quilted saddle pad, place it underneath the new saddle, and girth up. If you merely want to sit in the saddle without making any marks on it, do not put your stirrup leathers on yet. Get a leg up or use a mounting block and see where your seat naturally falls.

If you have a secure seat position, ride in the saddle (without adding your stirrups) until your horse has produced a little sweat under the pad. Then remove the saddle and the pad, and examine the sweat marks on the horse's back. A saddle that has even pressure will show it by having even sweat marks where the saddle was. If there was uneven pressure, you will see dry spots underneath the saddle pad where the saddle did not connect with the horse's back.

Don't expect more saddle padding to help make the saddle fit better. If a saddle has a wide tree, an extra pad may help, but if the tree is too narrow, the extra pad will only add to the pressure felt by the horse, particularly at the withers.

If the saddle passes this test, put your leathers on (it is a good idea to still protect the new saddle by wrapping the leathers with polo wraps or Vet Wrap) and climb aboard. Feel how your leg falls with the stirrup bars. Assess the overall picture: the deepness of the seat, the design of the flap, the fit of the twist, the position of your leg in the irons.

If you are truly interested in this particular saddle, ride in it more than once before making your final decision. It may feel strange to you, especially if you have only ridden in flat hunt-seat saddles or have been surrounded by yards of western leather for many years. You will know when the saddle fits well by its comfort and by the way it enhances your ride overall.

Breaking in the Saddle

Most dressage saddles are already supple and soft when they come from the manufacturer, and only need to be cleaned and conditioned in order for them to break in well. Usually a saddle will come with literature that explains how to care for it according to the manufacturer's specifications.

A few saddles—particularly "economy" saddles—have stiff leather. Others may have been on the showroom floor for a while and may have dried out a bit. Such a saddle should receive a light initial oiling in order to break it in properly and extend its life.

To oil your new saddle, you will need a can of leather dressing, a small container or bowl, and a soft paintbrush (natural bristle or foam, about one inch wide). The dressing is formulated to protect and soften new leather right away, but it will also replenish the moisture in older leather. It is usually

(continues)

easily absorbed by new leather. Apply the dressing to both sides of the leather. The saddle flaps will be most porous on the inside, so pay close attention to getting them well oiled. Let the dressing soak in completely. This will take anywhere from twenty minutes to an hour or more. Apply a second coat of dressing. The more dressing that is absorbed by the saddle, the more easily the saddle will break in. You can assist the break-in period by rolling the saddle flaps gently, suppling them with your hands. After your saddle has had its initial oiling, you will only need to clean and condition the leather for its routine care.

Your saddle, if it is quality leather, will start to take the shape of your horse's back after it begins to break in. This will add to your horse's comfort.

You should treat your leather saddle as you would your own skin. It needs to be cleaned and moisturized. Cleaning prevents sweat, dirt, and molds from getting onto your horse's skin and also protects the leather itself. Use a mild soap and a small, damp sponge to remove the dirt and grime. Then follow up with a leather conditioner to replace the good moisture that keeps leather supple. Never leave your saddle in direct sunlight or store it near extreme heat or in a cold, wet place. You don't want your saddle to dry out, but you don't want it to develop mold or mildew, either.

The Bridle

Thankfully, choosing a bridle and bit for your horse to train and show in is not as difficult or as expensive as saddle-buying, but certain regulations have to be followed. According to AHSA rules, at the lower levels (Introductory through Third, and optional at Fourth Level), dressage horses wear a plain snaffle bridle with a smooth snaffle bit. However, this description is pretty broad. You can choose from a variety of snaffles, but not every one is automatically approved for showing.

Because there are so many types of snaffles to choose from, it pays to understand which ones are allowed in competition, even if you never plan to show. AHSA rules are not based on fashions or trends, but instead have been selected because dressage riders and trainers over the years have found snaffles to be ideal bits for the sport's training objectives.

In contrast, Fourth Level through Grand Prix, the upper levels, use the double bridle. The double bridle works with two bits: a light snaffle, called a bradoon, and a curb. The curb bit exerts pressure on the bars of the horse's mouth as well as the chin groove and the horse's poll, causing him to lower his head, tuck in his nose, and flex at the poll and lower jaw. The bradoon works to raise the horse's head by slight upward pressure on his mouth. Because of the precise, sophisticated nature of this bridle, it is saved for the upper levels of dressage.

This is why the snaffle is used in lower levels. The snaffle alone is very direct in its action. The ends of the mouthpiece are attached to the rings directly, and the reins attach to the bit ring as well. While there is no leverage action with a snaffle as there is with a curb bit, the effect a snaffle has on the mouth varies according to the design of the mouthpiece. The effect also differs according to whether or not the bit has rings or cheeks. The mouthpiece itself may have one joint in the middle, or two, joined by a flat central link. There are unjointed snaffles with solid mouthpieces, too.

It is important to know the sensitivity of your horse's mouth as well as the size of his mouth. While most equestrians believe that snaffles are mild bits, any bit can be harsh in the wrong hands. For instance, don't assume that your delicate, small-mouthed Arabian will go better in a fat, rubber-coated snaffle. He may not be able to manage the large size. Choose a bit that is a proper fit both ways, with the mildest action you can find and in the correct width for his mouth.

Types of Snaffles
Here is a sampling of snaffles and what they are designed for:

MULLENMOUTH SNAFFLE   This bit is unjointed and slightly curved. Its action is very basic: it works entirely on the horse's tongue and lips. It may not be a good bit for a horse that likes to play with the mouthpiece because he can often push the bit up with his tongue. Since it has no joints, some horses find it uncomfortable because there is not enough room for the tongue.

LOOSE-RING SNAFFLE   The mouthpiece of this bit is attached to rings, but the rings are not fixed. When pressure is applied to the loose-ring, the bit moves to the most effective position on the tongue and bars of the mouth. Additionally, many horses like being able to chew their mouthpiece and move it around. A loose-ring snaffle encourages the horse to relax his jaw and is considered to be a good bit to use when starting a young horse. Some say that the loose-ring snaffle encourages the horse to accept the bit more readily because when he chews it, it produces saliva.

EGGBUTT SNAFFLE   The mouthpiece of this bit has T-shaped ends, which are designed to prevent the corners of the horse's mouth from getting caught or pinched. The shape of the rings helps prevent the bit from getting pulled through the mouth. Eggbutt snaffles are considered mild bits and have a fairly steady feel in the horse's mouth. Unlike the loose-ring snaffle, this fixed bit prohibits the horse from moving it as easily and therefore applies pressure directly to where the bit sits on the bars of the mouth and the tongue.

FULL-CHEEK SNAFFLE   This bit is designed so that it cannot be pulled through the horse's mouth. To keep the bit positioned on the tongue, so that pressure is applied properly, a full-cheek bit can be worn with leather bit-keepers that attach to the bridle's cheekpieces. Because the long cheekpieces put pressure on the horse's cheek, these bits are recommended as stronger bits for willful horses that are difficult to turn or steer. Half-cheek bits, an alternative to the full-cheek, also serve a similar purpose.

DR. BRISTOL AND FRENCH LINK SNAFFLES   Unlike the single-jointed snaffles, these bits have double joints, with a flat link in the middle. If you have a horse that has a fussy mouth or even a small mouth, he may find a French link or Dr. Bristol more comfortable. The French link is considered mild, but while the Dr. Bristol is similar in design, when placed in the horse's mouth with the middle joint perpendicular to the tongue, the bit has a very severe, blade-like action on the tongue. Also, if the horse does put his tongue over a Dr. Bristol, he may not be able to get it underneath the bit again, which will also cause him pain.

According to AHSA rules, all the parts of the bit that come in contact with the horse's mouth must be made of the same metal. An alloy, such as German silver, Aurigan, or stainless steel, is considered to be one metal and is therefore permitted. However, bits that incorporate another metal, such as copper rollers, "life-savers," or keys on a stainless-steel bit, are not allowed at shows. At the lower levels, the bit can be covered with rubber or can be made entirely of a synthetic plastic material.

Also not allowed at the lower levels is any bit with a port, twisted or wire, or a roller, or that works on leverage with a curb strap or chain, such as a Pelham or Kimberwicke. Any snaffle that is not smooth-mouthed, such as the slow-twist, corkscrew, or wire-twist, or is designed with holes in it is prohibited.

Next, Nosebands

A regular cavesson noseband should fit the horse snugly, but you should be able to get two fingers underneath the band and the horse's jaw. The band should lie midway between the corners of the horse's lips and his protruding cheek bones (about two fingers' width, just below his cheek). According to AHSA rules, the noseband must be made entirely of leather or leather-like material, although decorative metal on the outside is permitted, providing it doesn't protrude through the surface to the inside. Chain-lined or tack nosebands are prohibited.

A loose-ring snaffle with a regular noseband—a mild combination—is suitable for many horses.

If you have no need for anything other than a regular noseband, you can adjust it to emphasize or de-emphasize your horse's head. For example, a broad leather noseband can make a large head appear smaller. If your horse has small or delicate features, choose a slender noseband that is rolled or stitched so as not to overwhelm his face.

A full-cheek snaffle used without keepers.

Other nosebands are designed for different purposes. When fitting a special-purpose noseband, remember that whatever style you choose, you've got to adjust it correctly or else it will not be able to do its job. Also, keep in mind that trying to remedy a horse's fussy mouth by just cranking it closed may result in other problems. Forcing some horses to keep their mouths closed may cause them to set their jaws against the bit, thus making them become resistant to the bit instead of accepting it.

DROPPED NOSEBAND This noseband prevents the horse from opening his mouth too wide and therefore evading the action of the bit. It transfers the action of the snaffle from the corners of the mouth to the bars of the lower jaw. This noseband should be fitted on the end of the nasal bone, only slightly lower than where the cavesson noseband rests. The underside should fit around the outside of the bit, resting in the chin groove and buckling on the left, just below the bit. You should still be able to slide a finger all around the straps

A loose-ring snaffle with a dropped noseband. Notice that the noseband adjusts over the nose as well as under the chin to ensure better fit.

between the leather and the horse's head. A dropped noseband helps the bit to remain in the right position, resting on the horse's tongue and the bars of the lower jaw, so that the rider's rein aids are received. If the noseband is fitted too low, it will restrict the horse's breathing. Dropped nosebands that adjust across the nosepiece make it much easier to fit the horse correctly.

FLASH NOSEBAND   This noseband is a regular cavesson with a thin leather strap that threads through a loop on the front of the noseband, in front of the bit and underneath into the chin groove. The flash buckles on the left side. It also discourages the horse from opening his mouth and works on the same principle as the dropped noseband so that the horse must yield to the bit and relax at the poll. The flash shouldn't interfere with the horse's breathing. A poorly fitting flash will pull down the noseband at the horse's bridge.

A flash noseband with an eggbutt snaffle.

FIGURE-EIGHT NOSEBAND This noseband has two straps that cross over at the bridge of the horse's nose. The figure-eight noseband is made to discourage the horse from evading the action of the bit. The horse feels pressure on his nose and chin groove if he attempts to open his mouth to get away from the bit. It should be adjustable so that the upper buckle is just under the jaw and cheek and the lower buckle comes down at a sharp angle from the crossover point at the top.

JAWBAND CAVESSON The design of this cavesson allows the noseband to be tightened for more control of the horse. The strap underneath the chin cranks together to keep the horse's mouth completely closed. This noseband prohibits the horse from opening his mouth at all.

CRESCENT NOSEBAND This noseband is designed for the horse that is very strong and pulls his rider around. It has two flat metal loops that fit underneath the bridle's bit rings. It

The crescent noseband is designed for the horse that is very strong and pulls against the rider. The horse cannot avoid the pressure of the bit when wearing a crescent.

buckles in front of the bit in the chin groove and behind the bit, where the cavesson normally closes. The design affects the bridge of the horse's nose as well as the lower jaw. The horse cannot avoid the pressure of the bit when wearing a crescent.

Whatever equipment you choose, make sure that you are happy with the end results. If you try one noseband and bit combination and it doesn't have the desired affect, try an alternative combination. It's a good idea to borrow a noseband or bit from another rider to see if it works; otherwise, you may end up with a tack room full of extra leather and metal!

Meeting Other Enthusiasts

Now that you are all set up, you will definitely enjoy getting involved with other riders who share your enthusiasm for this sport. In many ways it helps to have the support and encouragement of people like yourself. One surefire method of finding dressage riders is joining your local dressage chapter or club. Most chapters sponsor a variety of clinics as well as put on a show series with year-end awards and hold monthly get-togethers for their members.

But how do you locate these fine people in your area? First, contact your state dressage association to find out where the local chapter is and who organizes it. You can find out the location of your state chapter by calling the USDF. You can also contact your state horse council to find out about different organizations that include quadrille (musical ride) teams or freestyle groups.

And on the subject of USDF, you may find it wise to join. The mission of the USDF is to promote excellence in horsemanship through dressage. This organization's objective also reflects the desire to further the cause by providing enthusiasts and riders with educational programs, events, and awards. If you join your official state dressage chapter and the chapter is a Group Member Organization (GMO), you may receive an individual membership to the USDF, which entitles you to rider awards, newsletter mailings, bulletins, and a discount on a subscription to *Dressage and CT,* the official magazine of the USDF. If you wish to compete in the Horse Awards, Breed Awards, or USDF/ABIG (American Bankers Insurance Group) Championships, you must join USDF as a participating member and register your horse. Often if you join your state dressage chapter, you can sign up as an affiliate member of the American Horse Shows Association for a small additional fee. While you will not be a voting member of the AHSA, you will be able to show at AHSA shows as a member. The address of the United States Dressage Federation is Box 6669, Lincoln, NE 68506-0669.

Need Extra Help?

If there's a strong dressage contingency in your equine community, you're lucky, but if you are finding only limited equipment and information, you will still be able to get the items you need in other ways.

Most tack shops will special order items for you, and ordering by mail from discount tack catalogs is another option.

If you're looking for videos, you can check for tack shops and national services that rent them. Many rental outfits will even send you items by mail. Many state dressage chapters have libraries so you can check out reference material by mail (sometimes for a small fee), and then you can sit and watch to your heart's content.

Check out the opportunities for dressage enthusiasts in cyberspace. Online services have sections devoted to equestrian endeavors, and you can meet people via the Internet.

Check out the opportunities in cyberspace, too. Every major online service has sections devoted to equestrian endeavors, and you can make friends via the Internet. You can participate in horse forums, where you can ask and answer questions about all kinds of equine topics. You can even buy and sell goods. Some fun "get-togethers" include live chatting on a particular topic or having a well-known equestrian answer questions online. Dressage groups often have newsletters or articles online that you may find helpful when you're just starting out.

Meeting people via your computer is fun, but getting a network of riders together in person helps build solid bonds among friends. If you're interested in organizing a small dressage club, post a sign advertising a meeting at the local tack or feed store, plan an agenda, and see what develops. You may just start out small, with only a few people, but having individuals who are willing to meet to share their common interest will make your experience all the more enjoyable.

Finding the Right Riding Instructor

Chapter Four

*I*n America, any individual can call himself or herself an instructor or trainer and receive fees for teaching the rider or riding the horse. It is very different in Europe, where most countries have trainer certification programs that interested candidates must complete in order to teach others. Many metropolitan areas in the United States will have several instructors to choose from, and it can be difficult to know how to select a quality instructor.

This is why the USDF has developed its Instructor Certification Program. The organization is working diligently to develop a program that takes the best of the European methods and incorporates them into valuable information for American instructors. Individuals who want to be certified must go through a stringent program that is developed to bring out the best in our teachers. Only the most dedicated, determined, talented individuals with clear-cut goals come out of the program certified.

Available nationally since 1990, the USDF Instructor Certification recognizes two types of certification: Training through Second levels, and Training through Fourth levels. As the sport grows, so does the demand for well-qualified teachers. The USDF offers many educational programs so that interested instructors can learn theory and practical application of riding, longeing, judging, and dressage history. Seminars, held annually for aspiring instructors, are designed to act as practice sessions for those who are preparing for their final evaluations.

Individuals who are testing for certification must undergo several hundred hours of preparation to demonstrate a high level of skill not only in riding, but also in teaching students. They must show that they can effectively communicate with students, determine what their problems are, and work out solutions for them. The program stresses safety overall, and because of this emphasis, it develops instructors who know how to use equipment correctly and avoid hazards so that the horse and rider's safety is never compromised.

Getting Started

When you start looking for a riding teacher, above all, seek out someone you are comfortable with to teach you and your horse. Not every teacher must ride FEI level in order to be a great instructor. Some of the very best teachers may only be a few levels above you, but they may be gifted communicators who can help you understand the fundamentals and eventually help you move on—perhaps beyond their level.

Begin your search by contacting the USDF for a list of certified instructors. Similarly, you can contact the American Riding Instructor Certification Program for an instructor that has gone through its training program (ARICP, P.O. Box 282, Alton Bay, NH 03810, 603-875-4000). However, there may not be an instructor available in your area who has participated in a USDF or ARICP program. You may have to do more research to find a qualified professional who meets your needs.

If this is the case, your best bet is to attend local dressage shows and observe instructors with their students. Watch the

In your initial search for an instructor, attend shows and watch teachers with their students. Observe the style of teaching and then match it with the scores of the students.

style of teaching and then compare it with the scores of the students. Was there any one teacher whose methods you felt were compatible with your ability to learn? Were there trainers who you felt were too intimidating for your personality? A good instructor will be focused on the student at the show—it is what the student pays for. A trainer who is off talking with fellow teachers or working her own string of horses may not be attentive enough for your needs.

Also, check with your local dressage chapter to see if they can provide you with a list of instructors in the state or in your area. Follow up by calling the instructor and letting her know your intentions. Ask if she minds if you watch one of her lessons to get a feel for her teaching style. A good trainer will welcome this type of "interview"—some trainers who value their current clientele's privacy may decline to do

To get a feel for a potential instructor's teaching style, ask if you can watch one of her lessons.

this, however. You'll have to decide how much of this refusal is ego and how much involves protecting their current clients.

When you evaluate a potential instructor giving a lesson, observe the session from a number of aspects. Check to see if the student is on time, ready to go, appropriately dressed and warmed up for the session. This will show you that the instructor has set parameters for the lesson program and the schedule is not just "loosely based" on a particular time. A good instructor will have taught the student how to place protective wraps or legwear on her horse and how the equipment should fit. If you see a horse going into a lesson with loose polo wraps or a saddle with the pad scrunched underneath it, it will detract from the lesson and show you that the teacher may not put much emphasis on the safety or comfort of horse or rider.

Check to see that the instructor arrives on time for the scheduled lesson. If the previous lesson ran overtime, which may happen occasionally if the teacher has a busy schedule, make sure that the next student doesn't have to pay with her session to make up for lost time. An instructor who lets the next student on her roster know she will be five or ten minutes behind schedule is still a very conscientious person.

When you observe the lesson, make a mental note of any training devices that the instructor may use and whether they are implemented properly. You may not be able to determine if they are being used appropriately, but you can probably tell if the horse is uncomfortable. If the instructor is using draw reins on one particular horse, there may be no cause for alarm, but if every horse in her barn is worked with some particular restrictive device, you may question these methods.

Observe how she explains riding theory. Does she use a lot of buzz words or jargon that means little to you? Does she explain a technique in more than one way so that the student has a grasp of what is expected? Is the delivery of information given in a positive manner, or does the teacher berate the student until she finally gets it right? Does the teacher get in the arena and watch, or does she take a spot on the sidelines and bark out commands as the student passes? Finally, does she

A good instructor will be able to help the rider understand concepts by demonstrating techniques in ways that are easily comprehended.

The instructor should be properly dressed so that she can ride the student's horse at any session.

reward the student for any positive reaction to her instruction, or does the student wonder if she's done it correctly?

Does the teacher go into the arena to demonstrate visually (even getting on the horse), or does she just speak from outside the rail? Is she properly dressed in case she must ride the student's horse?

A good riding instructor has a working knowledge of not only riding, but also of horse care management, feeding, proper fitting of tack, show etiquette, and business management. If you have settled on one or two particular trainers, speak with their students to get a feel for how satisfied they are. Ask the trainer for her references first, but don't try to go behind her back. She may just have you talk to individuals while you are at her training facility. Some of her students will probably be available to talk to you on the day you observe the lesson.

A good instructor will be happy to speak to you about any training issues you may have. She might not want to be your best friend, but she should enjoy discussing her work and riding program with you.

The instructor should also enjoy working around horses. This may seem like an obvious point, but as in other professions, teachers can suffer from job burn-out, and it will reflect in the way they handle their horses. Find out if the teacher still rides and competes herself. Ask if she also takes lessons or works with a coach from time to time and attends clinics or symposiums. Keeping her own knowledge fresh is a good sign that she is still enthusiastic about her work.

A good teacher will keep a solid schedule and be organized about it. This will lead to many happy returns down the road. A disorganized trainer will cause a great deal of grief due to missed appointments, poor billing habits, and the like. An organized trainer will make good use of her time and will not be a burden to those pupils who are also on a tight schedule. There is nothing worse than being well prepared for a lesson, only to have to wait for the teacher to show up.

An instructor who has a good working knowledge of all applications of tack and equipment is definitely an asset. Furthermore, if this person uses the least amount of equipment to

A good instructor should enjoy working around horses.

get the most out of her horses, so much the better. Heavy reliance on training gadgets shows little knowledge or application of the basics.

Finally, the instructor should be correct in her teaching principles. She can be the nicest person with a wonderful personality, but if she doesn't know what she's talking about, or does not have thorough knowledge of the discipline, you will not be spending your money wisely. This doesn't just apply to low scores in the show ring. Above all, dressage is correct training, and if the teacher doesn't have the classic principles down, your horse and you will be cheated out of a wonderful education.

How to Spot Trainer Burn-Out

If you have found several candidates, but have doubts about committing to their lesson program, it may be because you have seen signs that some of them may be unhappy on the job.

Instructors suffering from burn-out exhibit many of the common signs of this problem. They are late for work or may miss sessions altogether. They may have created an "overworked" situation, which manifests itself in them being stressed and uptight. A danger sign to look for is an instructor who seems to lose clientele often, with horses and riders coming in and out of her training barn. This person may fight with barn management frequently and voice displeasure about other trainers getting "special treatment." Instructors who are not concentrating on the job often spend time gossiping or just chatting away with rail birds during a student's lesson. Some may keep their lessons very short or begin to combine individual lessons into group lessons, spending less and less time at the barn. They may be full of excuses about why lessons are postponed, from weather conditions to footing problems to their own crises. Dangerous teachers are those who take out their frustrations on a horse in training and have angry outbursts that result in a battle or with the horse being beaten. Look for a different trainer when you see one who is relying heavily on training gadgets or bizarre methods.

Really distressed trainers often will be in poor health or may have personal habits or problems that can affect their work. Stay away from trainers who are dating any of their students! Finally, look at the health of the horses in their barn. Are they, for the most part, fit, sound, well fed and groomed, and free from major vices? If horses or riders are constantly "out of the game" due to lameness or accidents, it could be because the teacher pushes the students or horses beyond their capacity.

Different Types of Teachers

Finding a reputable, talented teacher is one thing, but ensuring that your learning style matches her teaching style is quite another. Meshing your personality with hers is often a tricky situation. While you don't really need your instructor to be your close pal, you do want to be on good terms with her and be able to learn from her. You need to observe her communication skills because a person who has the ability to ride a dressage horse well may not necessarily be able teach others to do the same.

Strict teachers will often drill their students, expecting accuracy and demanding discipline from their pupils. They may yell and sometimes even swear a blue streak when they see something that should be done correctly but isn't. If you are a strong person and do not mind when an instructor occasionally has outbursts while trying to drive a point home, then you will not have a problem with a strict instructor. Some students thrive in this type of regimented atmosphere. If, however, you tend to get discouraged by this type of treatment, find someone else whose approach is a little milder.

Find a teacher whose teaching style matches your learning style.

Some teachers use the same methods of correction and reward on students as they do on horses. You will hear these teachers immediately telling their students that they have done something properly, just as you will see them correct a bad situation quickly. Students who learn by positive reinforcement and repetition will seek out such teachers, who are often very enthusiastic about their programs.

Some teachers go a little too far in the other direction: they baby their students, and if students take advantage of the situation, they will learn very little. In typical lessons, most teachers do all the talking, but passive instructors can be an invitation to talk back for some strong-willed students. Often the teacher will make excuses for the student or for the horse, for example, "It's okay, the horse seems to be in a bad mood today." Students who are extremely meek may do fine with this type of trainer. Anyone who is dedicated to a serious training program will soon tire of this soft attitude, however. This kind of teacher might just want to be friends with her students and avoid any confrontation.

You may encounter teachers who don't want their students to rise to their potential and may want to try to "keep them down." They may be insecure about having a student surpass them, so they downplay a student's progress or success. If the student shows interest in moving beyond the teacher's capacity, the insecure teacher might keep the student coming back by not acknowledging her accomplishments. A student may not see what is happening until an outsider (even another trainer) sets her straight.

Set Up a Riding Appointment

Ask the potential instructor if you can set up a lesson or two. You'll have to bring your own horse if she doesn't have any lesson horses for you to ride, so find out what arrangements you will have to make and how much she charges for a single session. Then, during your own private session, use the criteria that you had for observing her pupils. By the end of the lesson, you will have your observations, your riding program "interview," and your riding session to help you make up your mind.

Instruction Versus Training

Although many American riders use the terms interchangeably, an instructor is different from a trainer. A trainer will actually ride and train your horse, while an instructor will be a coach for you. However, an instructor can also be a horse trainer, and you can determine if you would like your teacher to also teach your horse.

There are benefits to putting your horse in training when you are just starting out: The horse receives consistent training methods when the trainer rides. If you feel that you are sometimes muddling through, confusing your horse with inconsistent aids, the trainer can reinforce the basic principles with certainty. Also, you can watch the trainer ride your

Signs of a Great Instructor

- Never compromises the safety of horse or rider. Knows the appropriate use of equipment so that it never becomes a hazard.

- Knows that each horse and rider has a unique set of requirements. Understands that not every horse or rider can be taught according to one formula.

- Adapts to situations and can adjust the day's lesson accordingly. If the horse is fresh or in high spirits, the instructor can see this and help the student deal with the situation, instead of only concentrating on the planned lesson.

- Communicates well and has the ability to say the same thing many different ways to ensure that the information is understood.

- Has a keen eye and is insightful. She knows when the horse is going to get sluggish or blow up and can help the rider understand how to feel these things out.

- Encourages the rider without coddling her.

- Gives the rider confidence instead of taking it away.

- Uses positive commands to explain or correct: "Keep your elbows loose," not "Don't keep locking your elbows!"

- Challenges the rider to test her current level of skill but does not overface her so that she loses all desire to do it correctly.

- Asks for 100 percent from her students so that they can see results.

(continues)

- Teaches more than riding, for example, offers clinics on horsemanship like grooming and wrapping legs or how to longe the horse properly.

- Has enough confidence in herself to allow her riders to go to clinics taught by other instructors, to help broaden the students' knowledge.

- Knows when to move the student along to another teacher at a higher skill level, should the pupil exceed her knowledge.

horse and gain knowledge about what you should be doing when you are in the saddle.

When putting your horse into the hands of a trainer, follow the same procedure as you would for locating an instructor. Watch him or her ride a variety of horses, and see if you like the person's demeanor with animals. Any trainer that uses "quick fix" methods or brute force should be avoided. She will not get positive results that last, and she can cause much more harm in the long run. Check references just as you would with an instructor.

There is no foolproof way to determine if your horse needs training. But there are some red flags that can make your decision easier:

- If you are working with a young horse

- If you are working with a green horse

- If you are trying to change your horse over from a discipline that may have used conflicting training methods

- If your riding ability seems to be confusing your horse rather than making him understand what you ask

When putting your horse into the hands of a trainer, watch her ride a variety of horses and see if you like her way with them.

- If you do not have the time it takes to reinforce your lessons with your horse

Certification

Any rider who thinks that it is easy for a teacher to become USDF certified should think again. Instructors must be current USDF participating members and age twenty-one or over before they can apply for testing. A four-part application that documents past experience and accomplishment in riding, teaching, and dressage education must be filed. The application must also be accompanied by references.

Any qualified instructor may apply to take the exam. However, instructors that have attended pre-certification clinics, instructor seminars, USDF workshops, and other development courses are given preference. Only a limited number of candidates are selected to test, so the ones selected are the best instructors applying.

The USDF offers certification in two categories: Training through Second Level, and Training through Fourth Level. Each candidate must complete a five-phase exam. In order to be certified, the candidates are required to ride two lower level horses, longe one horse, longe one rider, teach two private lessons, teach one group lesson of three students, and take a verbal and a written exam. The second category requires the same, plus they must teach two private lessons to Third or Fourth Level students and ride two Fourth- or Prix St. Georges–level horses, one in a snaffle, and one in a double bridle. They have more extensive questions to answer on their oral and written tests.

In order to become a USDF-certified riding instructor, a candidate is required to ride two lower level horses, longe one horse, longe one rider, teach two private lessons, teach one group lesson of three students, and take a verbal and a written exam.

Volunteer students participate in the certification program, bringing their own horses and riding in real lessons. The sessions are generally thirty minutes long and conducted under the eye of an examiner, who is usually one of the top dressage trainers or riders in the nation.

The candidates must demonstrate to the examiners that they have the subject knowledge and skill to communicate that information to the students. The instructors' teaching skills are graded on a score sheet that lists the different criteria that add up to being a good teacher. They must demonstrate that they have shown concern for the safety and fit of the student's tack. They must be able to assess and identify both the rider's and the horse's problems. The instructors must then give appropriate exercises for the riders to perform, and they will be graded on the success of the exercises as appropriate. They must use the correct classical theory as the basis for their teaching. The USDF grades the instructors on their rapport with the student. It looks for a positive, not adversarial style—teachers who interact well with the student. The teachers must have a professional demeanor and present their lessons in a clear, loud voice, and use proper grammar and diction. Finally, the lesson's organization and focus are graded. All this is evaluated in the thirty-minute session.

The Instructor Agreement

Many instructors will give you a written agreement that outlines all policies that should be adhered to. The agreement will usually include payment terms, any additional expenses (show fees), and a release of liability. Your instructor may offer different payment schedules, depending upon the type of lessons you take. She may set rules on whether you must wear a safety helmet during lessons.

The Training Agreement

Your training agreement can be a very basic document, but it should outline some particulars to protect both you and your instructor. The language does not have to be difficult to understand; it should just cover the areas that you feel are the most important. If your trainer has a document that is very broad-based and you would prefer to add some details, simply ask to amend it, or work on an agreement together.

The training agreement should discuss **fees** and what they entail. It should note due dates on fees and if there will be late penalties if fees are not paid by that day. It should also cover fees for extra services.

It should include the **number of times** the horse is to be ridden by the trainer.

If it is an instructor's package, then it should include the **number of lessons** you are to receive.

It should note that the horse may be **handled** (or even ridden) by someone other than the instructor/trainer. Many times, if the trainer has a large clientele, she will include language in her contract stating that her assistant will groom/hand-walk/longe/warm-up your horse.

It should note that riding is a dangerous sport and that you release your trainer from **liability** should something occur to you or your horse.

Sample

SANDY ARENA TRAINING
123 Piaffe Way
Dressage Town, USA

Owner's Name _____

Address _____

_____

Telephone _____ Daytime _____

In case of emergency, notify _____

Relationship _____ Telephone_____

Veterinarian _____ Telephone_____

Farrier _____ Telephone_____

Date _____

It is hereby agreed as follows: I, _____, being the owner/rider, place my horse _____ in training with Sandy Arena (trainer). I agree to pay $_____ on the first day of each month for that month's training. If payment is not rendered by the 10th of the month, I shall incur an additional $10.00 late fee.

I agree to pay for a full month's training, even if I decide to stop training before the end of the month. If inclement weather prohibits trainer from working with horse during the month (as in winter season), sessions will be made up as time and weather permit.

If, during the term of this agreement, I wish to cancel my training with Sandy Arena, or take the horse out of training for an extended period, I must provide notice of two weeks (14 days) in writing.

Prior to receipt of the horse described, Sandy Arena shall have procured appropriate care, custody, and control insurance protecting me against any losses due to fire, theft, death, or other disability arising from any injuries to said horse caused by gross negligence of Sandy Arena, or its employees. Sandy Arena will make available to me, upon request, proof of insurance.

I agree to hold harmless and release Sandy Arena and its employees from any and all legal liabilities and responsibilities due to any and all accidents or injuries sustained by me or my horse while in training._____(initials) I agree to hold harmless and release Sandy Arena and its employees from any and all legal liabilities and responsibilities due to ordinary negligence._____(initials)

I do further agree that except in the case of gross and willful negligence, I shall bring no claims, demands, actions, and cause of actions and/or litigation against Sandy Arena and its employees for any economic and non-economic losses due to bodily injury, death, or property damage or loss sustained by me or my horse in relation to training by Sandy Arena. This includes (but is not limited to) riding, longeing, turnout, handling, and trailering.

I agree, by signing this release, that I realize that horseback riding is a dangerous sport. I realize that a helmet is required to be worn by all riders under the age of 18 years and that it is recommended for all riders in training with Sandy Arena. I realize that Sandy Arena assumes no responsibility or liability as stated in the above paragraph. I do hereby give my permission for Sandy Arena and its employees to ride, exercise, handle, longe, and train my horse.

In case of illness or injury to my horse, I give permission to Sandy Arena and its employees to contact my veterinarian, or in case my veterinarian is not available, any veterinarian on duty to administer to my horse any treatments said veterinarian feels necessary until I can be contacted. I agree to pay in full any bills resulting from such emergency treatments. (In the future event that I am unable to be contacted, I have outlined provisions for my horse as to the limit of care it can receive, contact name in the event I cannot be reached, and what to do if it is a life-threatening situation.)

In case of my own accidental injury, I give permission to Sandy Arena and its employees to call 911 or any emergency service and further give permission to be treated by a doctor or hospital emergency room staff.

Insurance Carrier _____

ID Number _____

Preferred Physician _____

HMO (if applicable) _____

Monthly Training Fees and Schedules

Full Training: $320

Includes six sessions per week to be divided into lessons or schooling sessions, daily turnout, blanketing during winter, administering feed (cost of actual feed not included), longeing, mane pulling, applying standing wraps during evening, and any other services to be determined by owner and trainer.

Full Limited Training: $250

Includes five sessions per week to be divided into lessons or schooling sessions.

Half-Training: $150

Includes two sessions per week to be divided into lessons or schooling sessions.

Lessons: $25 per half-hour, private

Additional services

Mane pulling _____$15.00

Mane braiding _____$35.00

Clipping—trim _____$25.00

Body clipping _____$80.00

Tail pull/bang_____$20.00

Blanketing _____$25.00 monthly

Turnout_____$15.00 for 2x/week

Longeing _____$30.00 for 2x/week

I have read and do understand the foregoing agreement, warnings, release, fees, and prices. I further attest that all facts relating to the applicant are true and accurate.

Signature _____
Trainer's Signature _____
Date _____

Today's Liability Issues

Why so much fuss about liability? Why is it that you must sign your life away on a typical training or instructor's agreement? Because, unfortunately, lawsuits have become a way of life in the United States. Gone are the days when you could just have a verbal agreement and go about "business as usual." An instructor in America must carry her own liability insurance, which is costly. If there is litigation, her insurance company must provide an attorney and pay legal defense. In most cases, your instructor will want you to sign a release before beginning her lesson program, in the event that you are injured and may want to file suit later. However, you are entitled to ask your instructor or her employees to sign a release that gives *you* protection should she or one of her employees become injured while training your horse.

Horseback riding is a dangerous sport. Due to the inherent risks of equine activities, new laws are being drafted that will help protect equine professionals from lawsuits. Nowadays, though, you may need protection from complete strangers, too. How many times have you spotted an unfamiliar person at the front of your horse's stall, someone who just wants to "stop and pet" your horse or give him a carrot? Even if you have the world's most sedate, friendly horse, it's best to keep strangers away from him. Countless numbers of non-horsey people have been hurt because they were holding a carrot wrong and got bit, or the horse accidentally stepped on their foot, or they just thought it would be fun to hoist their little Sarah on your horse's back and she got bucked off!

Many instructors and trainers have added special considerations to incorporate safety and protect themselves and, in turn, you and your horse, from problems that might arise. A conscientious trainer:

- Inspects her facilities for hazards and eliminates anything that may injure people or horses.

- Does not use barbed wire for fencing and removes dangerous objects from walkways, pastures, and arenas.

- Keeps roadways in good repair.

- Has fire extinguishers in barn aisles.

- Does not allow smoking on the property.

- Has first-aid kits for horses and people.

- Has a message machine for emergencies and checks the machine at regular intervals.

- Has on the premises safety lighting that can be operated by a timer.

- Insists that students, regardless of age, wear approved safety helmets and has worked out an arrangement with a local tack shop for discounts.

- Posts warning signs to the public.

- Keeps facilities locked so that trespassers are discouraged.

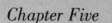

Chapter Five

Getting the Most Out of Lessons

O nce you've committed to beginning a lesson program, you'll soon find that your dressage lessons are structured a little differently from those of other riding disciplines. Dressage lessons can be pretty demanding, and they require you to think, react, and apply yourself. Your teacher may also require you to do "homework"—anything from a set of exercises in the saddle to extra reading material. You may not be accustomed to the sheer magnitude of information presented (not to mention the information available), but if you are enthusiastic about learning, you'll welcome the challenge.

It's important to note that any success you have with your lessons depends upon what you put into them. You can't slack off, because you will not see anything but meager results. And you can't merely sit on the horse and look nice, because appearance is far down the scale of importance. In dressage, the most crucial element is the way your aids effectively influence your horse.

Former hunt-seat riders are used to a regimen where the warm-up takes about fifteen to twenty minutes of walk-trot, reversing direction, then canter, then on to the important stuff—jumping. This is not to disparage hunter or jumper teachers, because many hunt-seat instructors do incorporate elements of dressage into their flatwork. But their main emphasis is usually on gymnastic exercises over fences and on the correct position.

Your hunt-seat riding style will have to be adjusted a bit. You have to learn another form of riding. Hunter riders often have to break the habit of "looking for their next fence" and twisting their torso when turning. They must get used to the fact that there's no "two-point" seat, no closed hip angle, no steering with the reins, and no jamming their heels down. If it is difficult during your lessons to make a break from your old riding routine, just let your instructor know. She will find alternative ways to establish new habits, and soon your new position will become more like second nature.

If you have a western pleasure-riding background, you'll know that it involves a heavy emphasis on equitation and the horse's headset. You have ridden with a deeper seat than a hunt-seat rider, but you haven't had much leg or rein contact with your horse. You are used to a different cadence in your horse's gaits, and soon you will discover exactly what "forward" means. If you didn't ride your horse in a snaffle, you'll have to learn two-handed rein contact. Much of your time in a western saddle may have been spent on style rather than function, so your new work will incorporate riding with a purpose.

Your New Lessons

You can look forward to a unique experience when working with a dressage instructor. A typical dressage lesson program will start with you on a longe line. Since your instructor wants you to develop an independent seat, she will put you on the longe so you don't have to worry about controlling the horse. Usually you will let go of the reins and for security hang on to a saddle strap fastened to the saddle's front rings. Some teachers will have the student on the longe working without stirrups or reins, to help the rider maintain balance at the walk, trot, and canter, along with all the transitions. Exercises with legs and arms will help deepen the seat, lengthen the leg, strengthen the stomach muscles, and improve balance. Once the rider has some security and control of the body, she can graduate from the longe. Longe-line lessons are also a super tune-up tool regardless of the student's riding experience. You'll learn a lot from these longe sessions, and you'll enjoy them too!

Regular riding lessons generally begin with warm-up at the walk on a loose rein. The horse is asked to move forward from behind before moving into the trot. The trot is also established

A typical dressage lesson program usually starts the rider on a longe line so she can develop an independent seat without worrying about controlling the horse.

on a loose contact. Then the rider begins to take up contact without losing the horse's energy and adds some figures into the warm-up, including 20-meter circles, serpentines, and change-of-rein across the diagonal. Canter work is then added, all the while working the horse to accept the bit and become relaxed and "through." Then the warm-up is over and the real work begins. Each instructor usually designs her own unique warm-up method to get horse and rider ready to take on the main task of the lesson.

Following your instructor's set lesson plan, you will work on a particular building block, for instance, impulsion or straightness. This becomes the focus of the exercises until you understand this element. Your instructor then adds to that, establishing your foundation. Once that is in place, your teacher can begin working with exercises and movements that may be found in dressage tests, including lengthening of the gait, leg-yielding, free walk, and shoulder-in.

Some instructors will evaluate the warm-up to determine that day's lesson. This allows her to see how the horse is behaving as well as determine what basics need to be reinforced.

Your instructor may prefer to evaluate your warm-up to determine what element needs work. Repetition of particular principles reinforces them and enhances your riding foundation. Evaluating your warm-up also allows your instructor to see how your horse is behaving so she can give you the tools to deal with the horse's temperament on that day.

Quality Lessons

Sometimes it is difficult to be objective about the training you are receiving, especially if you have established a bond with your instructor. But it is important to get correct, classical instruction if you are to make dressage your goal, regardless of whether you plan to show or not. There are ways to measure the success of your riding program that don't involve a judge.

If you are doing things the right way, you'll see it in your horse. You will notice that your horse's musculature is developing in the correct areas: over the topline and neck, through the haunches, and in the shoulder. After workouts, his muscles will be soft and supple in the hind end. On the other hand, if your horse develops soft-tissue injuries or mild lameness, he may be getting pushed too early for his development. Similarly, if he exhibits stress-related behavior, such as not eating, stall vices, or barn sourness, he might be unable to handle the heavy mental requirements of the sport, and you may have to slow your schooling schedule down. If he behaves as though he dreads the time he must spend in the arena, you may have to rethink your riding program or your teacher.

Because of your training, your own muscles will begin to strengthen through the thigh, in the abdomen, through the back, and even in the arms. You'll probably experience sore muscles, but there is a difference between well-worked muscle and fatigued tissue. If you are constantly sore, whether in the muscles, your spine, or other bones, your riding position may not be correct (or may not be encouraged to be correct).

If you are falling off more than staying on, you can lay odds that your instructor should be paying better attention to your seat. She may have to put you back on the longe line. If, however, you are surviving a skittish, nervous horse's antics better than you ever did before, you are probably improving your balance, seat, and reflexes!

If you have any doubts as to the quality of your training or the methods of your teacher, confide in a dressage friend from your network. Double check with books and magazines to see if what you are being taught is indeed correct. If you find that the training methods match what you are reading, then you'll know that your time and money are being well spent, and you can relax. If all signs point to something less positive, find a way to discuss this with your teacher before making any drastic moves.

Don't schedule lessons with a different teacher right away to compare the two. Most teachers have their own unique methods and way of communicating similar principles. You may wind up confused if you immediately run to another teacher to try to see which one is correct.

Frequency of Lessons

How often you take lessons depends upon your schedule and your budget. Having a lesson does not just take a one-hour block of time since you need to tack up, warm up, learn, review, cool down, and put up your horse. Allow about three hours for all of this activity.

Establish the best time of day for you to take lessons. Is your horse close enough to work that you can just go over to the stable and ride after a day at the office? Or are you so busy during the week that you can only take a lesson on the weekend? If you're not a morning person, scheduling lessons before work is a big mistake, and if you are exhausted by the time you finish work, you will not be prepared mentally or physically for a demanding after-work session.

Lessons can be costly, so see how your schedule and budget can handle them.

It's important to determine the best way that you learn material. Are you the type of person who can take with you the memories of the session, make mental notes, and apply what you learned later on during the week? Or do you tend to forget everything the moment you exit the driveway of the barn? Some people need the extra support that multiple lessons provide, while self-motivated individuals can handle less frequent lessons. Determine what your learning curve is and what lesson schedule you need.

Next comes money. Lessons can be costly, particularly in metropolitan areas where instructors can charge upwards of forty dollars per lesson for an hour's time. Generally, instructors will provide clients with "packages" so that if they buy a particular number of lessons per month, the cost is reduced considerably. For instance, an instructor may offer a lesson package that gives the student two forty-five-minute private lessons per week for two hundred dollars. This works out to approximately twenty-five dollars per lesson in a four-week period, which is economical for the student.

If you keep your horse at home and are going to trailer to an equestrian facility for lessons, you need to figure into your total lesson expenses the cost of hauling your horse to the lesson site. In this case, it may be better to cut down the number of sessions but lengthen the time of the session to get as much out of the lesson as possible. Occasionally, instructors will travel to your home to give you private lessons, but while this may save you hauling time and money, you will often have to pay a premium for that type of service.

Still, there are ways to help make the use of your time and money as efficient as possible. If you are thinking about having a private lesson on your own property, you can inform other interested pupils in the neighborhood who can hack over for their own session, making the trip more worthwhile for the instructor and perhaps reducing the cost of the lessons. You'll also benefit from watching the other sessions in your own backyard.

If you need to have a lesson nearly every day but have not yet won the lottery, it may be beneficial to have a friend videotape your lesson. This way you can take your session home and study it. Videotaped lessons help you review the elements taught to you and possibly help with your "homework" between lessons. Have a pad and pencil handy during your viewing, and take notes on important points. Then take your notes with you to the barn the next time you ride.

Riding in a Dressage Arena

Your sessions at home can be more effective if you ride in an arena set up for dressage. Many riders quickly understand the value of riding in an arena with the correct dimensions after seeing how their 20-meter circles practiced in the open are often egg-shaped or their serpentines are uneven. You can set

A sturdy arena setup is a combination of proper land preparation, excellent footing, and durable arena markers.

up a practice arena with the correct dimensions to enable you to work on your figures properly and get a good feel for the geometry.

The dressage arena, often called a court or manège, can be either 20 by 40 meters (66 by 131 feet) or 20 by 60 meters (66 by 198 feet). The arena wall is not really a wall at all, but usually just a rail connected to each marker. Often a dressage arena will be set up within a larger arena so that riders can ride around the perimeter before entering at A.

It is not known for certain what the letters that are used as markers stand for. Many theories abound, but the mystery of the letters continues to spark debate and plenty of guessing.

Letters are placed with precision, with the two end letters at the center of the short side (at 10 meters). The corner letters are 6 meters from the end letters. Space in between letters on the long sides is 24 meters. Since 3.28 feet equal 1 meter, you can use a multiplication formula with a standard

100-foot tape measure. Measuring kits that have cable labeled with the correct dimensions are available and eliminate guesswork.

Setting Up Court

You have options for setting up your own schooling area, whether you are at home or at a boarding facility. Your boarding stable probably would not be the place to set up a permanent arena, but you can mark off the dimensions (get permission, first) in order to train accurately. You can purchase red cones from an auto supply store or home-improvement store and paint the letters of the manège on them. You can also order them ready-made from tack catalogs. Place the cones inside the riding center's arena; use a tape measure for accuracy.

If your barn manager is agreeable, he or she might let you hang up lettered placards around the ring so that you don't

A simple way to mark off a dressage arena is with painted cones.

have to set them up and take them down for every ride. Showjumpers and western riders that board at the barn can use the letters as dressage riders do instead of calling out fence posts or light poles for transitions.

Building Your Own Arena

If you have the space and the desire to put together an arena on your own property, you'll need to do a little research before starting any construction. First, you need to determine a good location. Find an area on your property that is the most level so that you won't have to do much cutting and filling of the land. It should be on land that has good drainage and does not pool up with water during the rainy season. You know that you need at least 20 by 40 meters (for a short court), with 20 by 60 meters being ideal. Stake out the court and the perimeter. Next, you'll need to clear this plot of land of any vegetation.

Next, estimate the ground slope, which will help determine how well the plot drains. Be careful, because too much slope can actually cause strain on your horse's legs and can also cause too much soil erosion. The "slope" of the arena should not be detectable to the eye. To make sure that it is done correctly, have a contractor survey the slope by using a transit, which is part of a surveyor's equipment.

The maximum slope should be no more than 2 percent. Any more of a slope will make it difficult to work your horse effectively. Between 1 and 2 percent is beneficial, however, because rain water will drain off better. Your arena can slope from side to side, or it can come to a peak at the center, called a crown, where the water sheds off centerline and outside the perimeter.

The arena is made of three separate substances: sub-base, base, and footing. The sub-base is the very bottom layer, and it is made up of clay or stones. This foundation is packed down hard with a construction roller. The base, between the sub-base and the footing, should be about 4 or 5 inches deep.

A deeper base, such as 8 to 10 inches, is appropriate for jumping and other concussive sports, but it is too deep for dressage. The base acts as an anchor for your arena, keeping the surface footing in place. Your base should contain no stones and should be packed down as hard as you can get it. A contractor with a roller should be used once again to help you accomplish this. If you have any serious dips or hills, they can be filled or leveled at this time. If the arena base is uneven or inconsistently packed, the arena surface will also be uneven and inconsistent.

The reason you spend so much time preparing the bottom layer of your arena is to prevent the sub-base layer from working its way up to the top. If you simply pour a surface material on your land, you will be picking up rocks every time it rains or when the arena is turned over with a harrow. Also, arenas take a beating from hooves and harrows, so you want your surface to stay in the best shape possible. By packing down your sub-base layer and giving the arena a solid, well-set base, your surface will not erode away easily.

Choose your surface carefully according to your climate and your geography. Your footing should provide your horse with just enough cushion to reduce the impact of his weight on his legs, but it should stay firm enough to keep him from sinking down. The footing should have the same consistency throughout, with no hard areas or deep areas that might force him to compensate with choppy strides or uneven movement.

The footing for your arena should be about 3 to 4 inches deep, but no more than 5 inches. Most dressage riders like sand arenas, but you can prepare a mixture that fits your budget. There are natural materials such as sand, silt, sawdust, shavings, and mulch. There are also artificial, commercial footings that are made of everything from old athletic shoes to recycled tires. Many experts say that you should have your base tested by a state agricultural unit to see what it is composed of organically and then choose your footing based on the results. You may also want to check with local dressage riders and see what they are using as footing in their arenas.

You want to come up with a mixture that is not too hard or dusty, that doesn't get too deep or become too slippery when wet, and that doesn't freeze easily. Using a mix of dirt (which would include clay, soil, etc.), sand (whether from a beach or riverbank, or commercial or industrial sand), and sawdust or shavings can actually give you the footing that you desire at a good price. Sand by itself can often get too deep and put your horse in danger of leg muscle strain. Loose footing can cause tendon and ligament strain. Footing that is too hard does not distribute the concussion of your horse's gaits and can cause foot problems, such as sole bruises and even arthritis.

Some people use manure as their footing since it is free and readily available to horse owners. However, it becomes dusty and foul-smelling during hot, humid conditions, and during rain it can become slick and slippery. If manure is not composted thoroughly before spreading, it becomes a breeding ground for parasites and flies. Whenever possible, stay away from adding manure to your footing.

After you have experimented with your footing and have found a mixture that is suitable, you'll want to make the arena look like a dressage ring. At the high end of the price scale, you can buy polyvinyl fencing that comes pre-measured and ready to drop in place. But if you spend most of your money on the important stuff—the arena's surface—you'll probably be happy with an alternative to fancy boards.

For your rails, you can buy wooden two-by-fours. They should be sealed and kiln fired to resist warping. Otherwise, you can go to your local home center and buy 4-inch PVC pipe that is sturdy enough to go around the ring without too many dips. For your connectors, you can use cinder blocks and run both the wood or pipe through the top hole in the blocks and bury the bottom of each block. Or you can use wood posts inserted in the ground and nail your rails to them. Some creative builders use large plant containers, often

You can add railing in a variety of ways, including large plant containers with slots cut in them for PVC pipe rails.

You can set up arena markers by using plastic chains and lightweight stakes, which are available through catalogs.

bought in bulk from nurseries, and then cut a dip in the bottom of them to sink the pipe across. If you want the do-it-yourself type of ring but don't have the money for expensive fencing, many catalogs offer a set of plastic chains and posts that allow you to set up your arena in minutes and give your dressage court an elegant look.

Some stakes work well in almost any ground, but the longer the stake and the harder the ground the more difficult it will be to drive the stake in without bending it. If your ground is very hard (outside of your prepared arena), use a spike first and drive it into the ground, making a hole. Then place your stake in. The benefit of harder ground around your prepared arena is that your stakes will have a better chance of staying in place longer if you want to leave them up for a good length of time.

Maintain your footing intelligently. If you soak your arena, you'll end up doing damage to its base. If you don't water it enough, the footing may be dust in the wind. Keep the moisture level between 8 and 15 percent (a moisture meter for plants can be obtained at a nursery or garden center). Harrow the surface regularly to smooth it out or bring up the surface. Your horse will benefit if you maintain the arena regularly.

Cross-Training

The reasons that riders give for not cross-training are plentiful: "I'll ruin my horse if I take him out on the trail." "Forget about jumping—I'll just undo everything that I taught him earlier."

Nothing could be farther from the truth. If anything, cross-training should enhance your dressage schooling. In Europe, dressage riders often combine regular hacks across the countryside and jumping sessions with their serious training.

Jumping

If your horse already has a background in jumping, then the dressage work should enhance his ability over fences.

Remember, though, that unless you do a lot of regular jumping, your horse might be a little rusty as far as finding the perfect spot to the fence. He also might look at jumping as a type of release and get a little strong. Dressage supples and strengthens the horse, so he may feel as though he's got a little more spring over the jump. Let your horse relax and stay over lower jumps, such as crossrails, until they become just another stride.

You can then add variety to the jumps by going over painted "flower boxes," gates, oxers, and rails so that he gets a chance to be exposed to all types of obstacles.

Cavaletti

If you've never worked your horse over cavaletti, you will appreciate how it can help him in different ways: improving rhythm, developing better muscles, and improving gaits. Your horse should move more expressively with continued cavaletti work, and you'll feel the swing in his stride. Cavaletti work will improve your riding, too. It helps you learn to feel your horse's movement better, and you'll be able to follow the

Cavaletti, set up first as ground poles, offer a good introduction for basic trot or canter work, and when raised from the ground, they encourage the horse to lift his legs more.

motion of your horse. You'll stay better balanced, and your leg position will become more secure. If the horse goes through the cavaletti on a regular basis, he will develop his muscles evenly on both sides and loosen those muscles by lowering his neck and relaxing his back.

Cavaletti work often begins with a set of four ground poles and then moves up to cross-ended higher poles. The ground poles offer a good introduction to basic trot or canter work. Then when they are raised up from the ground, they encourage the horse to lift his legs more. You will need to evaluate your own horse's unique stride in order to find the best placement for your poles and then set them either for walk or for trot. Setting your poles up one at a time to introduce your horse gradually to the task will help if he's a little skittish. When you add a pole, place it about 3 feet from the first and then adjust it to your horse's stride. Limit your cavaletti to four poles maximum.

Teach your horse to walk and trot calmly through the cavaletti on a loose rein, then on contact, then in a "long and low" frame. These suppling exercises can work wonders for his mind and body.

If you want to get into cavaletti work seriously, there are books that will help you set up all kinds of exercises for your horse. Look for them at your local tack shop, bookstore, or library.

Gridwork

Gridwork, a gymnastic form of jumping, teaches the horse to be aware of his body and helps reinforce the rhythm of jumping for you. As the horse rocks back and forth during a combination of fences, you will find that you can concentrate on your position and your balance without having to worry as much about the horse actually taking the fence.

Grids are usually set up as lower fences and can involve a single stride between jumps or a "bounce" (jumps with no strides in between). You can set up poles as wings along the jump standards to reduce the chance of your horse running out of the grid, but most will eagerly finish all the jumps in a row.

Trail Work

Long-distance hacks or endurance riding will also help your dressage work. Horses can gain suppleness, tone, and muscle when ridden over hills and various surfaces. Hill work must be started at slower gaits and should be added into the horse's program in short, gradual sessions. Hills should not be too steep, but should be small and rolling. Riding up hills works different muscle groups than going down hills, so vary the pattern that you ride. Do hill work once or twice a week only, and space out your rides to keep your horse in good condition.

Trail riding not only helps horses gain suppleness, tone, and muscle when ridden over hills and various surfaces, but it also helps their mental attitudes.

Regular rides on the flat that incorporate lengthening, collecting, leg-yield, and extended walk improve the horse's responsiveness, too. Every horse will have his own strengths and weaknesses out on the trail. Some excel in going downhill, while others have the speed of a sprinter on the flat.

If you've never taken your arena-bound horse out on trail, he will probably be a handful or outright spooky, so introduce him to it slowly. Ride along with a very seasoned horse and rider to help smooth things over. On your first outing, simply take your horse for a walk and limit the time to a short jaunt. As the horse gets more accustomed to going out on trails, you can extend the time out, but continue to ride with a friend until your horse deals with the trail in a relaxed fashion. After a few sessions, your horse should lose that panicked look in his eye and will probably settle down and enjoy his time away from the ring.

When you are out on the trail, you will come across natural terrain that can help condition your horse, but pay attention to the footing. Ride on familiar trails so that you won't meet any surprises, such as ice, hard ground, deep mud, or rocks. For instance, if you decide to work on trot-to-halt transitions, don't do this in a slippery area. Also, if you take a friend with you, make sure that when you exercise at a faster gait there is enough room for the two of you on the path. Be sure your horse is warmed up so he does not pull muscles or strain tendons.

If you want to increase your horse's endurance with work on the trail, work with him to pace himself at the trot. At first, ride for a short distance (6 to 10 miles). Learn how to read his vital signs—pulse, respiration, and heartbeat—and how to observe him overall to determine when he's tired. Plan your outings so that you don't go on long rides on consecutive days.

Cross-Country

Jumping cross-country fences is another way to keep your horse keen and interested in his work. If you have never jumped outside of an arena, stick to very low fences to see how your horse behaves when jumping in the open. You will understand what it means to have a "forward going" ride if your horse really gets into it.

As with all kinds of cross-training, jumping cross-country fences is a different way for you to ride your horse so that he doesn't get sour or resentful. It will also help you as a rider because you will still ride with a deep seat as you do in dressage, not the equitation seat of the hunter ring. This secure jumping position requires a different type of balance and different leg muscles, so it will keep you on your toes— actually on the balls of your feet.

Always remember to go with another rider for safety. Otherwise, if you and your horse became separated while on a cross-country course, it could be hours before anyone found you.

Working on Your Own

If you are good at homework in between lessons, you can be aided by making notes—mental or actual—on your last lesson and trying to apply them when your instructor isn't there. Use repetition and rhythm to help you with your lesson's elements, and repeat them audibly: "Inside leg to outside rein, inside leg to outside. . . . "

Have your instructor help you develop a long-range goal to work toward. Settle on concepts that can be addressed at home, and focus on them. Work on areas that you feel need improvement, and don't feel as though you might be undoing all that you've learned in your lesson. Horses are very forgiving, and typically you won't ruin them if you make a few mistakes in between lessons. Try to concentrate on the feeling you had when your teacher told you that you were correct in your position or your execution of an aid. Once you begin to gain a feel for what is correct, you can make your work at home more worthwhile.

Maintaining Your Schedule

Chapter Six

*L*ike any demanding sport, dressage can be all-consuming, especially if you are very enthusiastic. But there are ways in which you can allow yourself to enjoy the sport without letting it take over all aspects of your life. Balancing a good training schedule and the rest of your life will not only reduce internal pressures but will also relax your external time constraints.

Some riders are fortunate enough to have fantastic schedules so that they are able to ride and spend time caring for their horses for hours on end every day. Many riders, however, have the opposite problem. They may want to devote a good deal of time to the sport, but due to a heavy work schedule or other commitments such as family, school, or other hobbies, they cannot find the time to get out and train as much as they'd like.

Most working people would agree that there is just not enough time during the day to get everything they want to accomplished. Therefore, it is important to your success in dressage to adjust your schedule so that you won't "fall behind in your studies" and can still keep the rest of your life running smoothly.

Remember, too, that you are not the only one involved in this, and even if you do have all the time in the world to get your horse out daily and school or take a lesson, you should take into consideration your horse's learning style, too. While you can stay as enthusiastic as you want, it is important to know how to tailor your sessions to your horse's needs so that they end up being fun and rewarding for both of you.

Developing a Schedule

When evaluating your ideal riding and schooling schedule, look first within yourself to see what type of person you are. Are you a night-owl, with more energy after your workday is over? Or are you completely exhausted after a long day at the office? Do you have a low energy period mid-afternoon? Are you someone who rises with the sun, alert and ready to go?

Determine how often you can school your horse by taking into consideration your schedule and obligations.

Then think about the logistics involving your horse. Is he kept at home? Is he boarded close to home? Do you have to travel long distances from work to get back to him at the end of the day? Or is he close enough to the office that you can visit him on your lunch break?

Now that you have determined your best times to ride, figure out how much "free time" you have in any given week.

Do you have to pick up kids from school, or are you taking classes after work? Do you have a relationship that requires a lot of time out of your schedule? Are you involved in any special committees or organizations that meet regularly? Do you have any standing appointments (hairdresser, chiropractor, dentist, etc.)?

Once you take all these elements into consideration, you will know how much time you can spend on your riding program. For example, a person who has enough energy after the workday to ride, keeps her horse near work, and has "free time" until 7:30 p.m. on weekdays can have an evening ride nearly every weeknight. However, if this same person keeps her horse near home, 25 miles away from work, she may not get to the stable in good time or be in the right frame of mind after sitting in traffic for hours. This person may have to schedule her serious riding for weekends and try to catch a ride only if traffic is light coming home, or if she leaves work early.

If you don't mind getting up early and riding before work—something especially nice if your horse is kept at home—you can head into the office afterward. Those who have flexible hours in the office can perhaps come in later in the morning and stay late in the afternoon as a compromise. Check with your employer about the possibility of arranging flex time if your company doesn't already have that policy. Many employers can be lenient about when you put in your hours, as long as a full workday is completed.

A rough estimate of how much time you'll need for your ride should include:

- Driving time both ways

- Grooming/tacking-up time

- Warm-up/work session/cool-down time

- Cleaning up, feeding

Stress and Your Riding

Stress has a negative effect on riding. Riders who have stressful events occurring in their lives often take out their anxiety on their horses. Even if they see their horse as a shoulder to cry on, stress makes the rider's body react in undesirable ways. Tense riders get stiff and develop poor riding positions. They communicate their tension to their horses so their aids are not effective. Some stressed-out riders express their agitation verbally, while others may hold it in and seethe. They may not be able to focus on the tasks at hand, which will also cause their schooling to suffer.

It's easy to become frustrated and stressed when your schedule doesn't go quite as planned, so find alternatives to compensate for the time lost. One of the best ways to avoid the stress of a heavy schedule and riding is to organize your time as best you can and prioritize your duties. Work, family, school, and home are all aspects of life that must be dealt with first. Don't sacrifice these things just so you can keep up with your riding schedule.

If your plans get shifted, see about an alternate time to ride. If there is only one block of time in which you can get to the barn, don't be frustrated because of the missed opportunity. Your schooling may have to come along more slowly because of your lifestyle, but that isn't a negative in itself. Don't let the important elements in your life suffer, as they are crucial in helping you develop into a well-rounded rider. For instance, those who neglect school or relationships because they would rather ride will eventually pay for it with poor grades or failing friendships.

If, however, you are trying to eliminate elements in your life that cause you grief, you can look at your riding time as a period that cannot be encroached upon by others—but only if you can make the conscious effort to leave the negatives outside of the arena. Above all, remain flexible, and don't take things too seriously when they don't work out as planned. Riding should be fun, so try to relax.

Physical Riding

As you take lessons and get into a steady routine, you'll begin to feel the effects of the sport on you. Dressage does not require brute strength, but it does require you to think of yourself as an athlete. Sore muscles can make a rider satisfied after a solid day's workout.

However, it can take its toll on you as well. If your endurance is compromised, you may feel exhausted after even a short ride. If you are really out of shape or significantly over your ideal weight, you will undoubtedly hurt from your day at the barn. Unfortunately, unless you can ride several horses each day, you will probably need to find another type of exercise program to help you keep up with the discipline's physical demands.

Different areas of your body need to become fit and toned in order to properly influence your riding, because your horse is not the only athlete participating in this sport.

ARMS AND SHOULDERS   Your arms should be soft and supple yet have enough muscle tone to apply a non-allowing rein during a strong half-halt.

LEGS   Your legs should be very strong, and the muscles should be elastic. Your thigh and calf muscles combine to engage, drive, and balance the horse. Your leg position also allows your seat to become deep.

BACK AND STOMACH   Your back and stomach support you and keep you in balance with your horse. Your stomach muscles help support your back so that it can both absorb the shock of the horse's movement and maintain your upright position. Your back muscles act as shock absorbers as well as "energizers" and also help deepen your seat.

Your stomach and back muscles together with your legs, arms, and shoulders help the horse develop self-carriage, which is the ultimate goal of dressage.

Your Personal Fitness Program

To increase your overall endurance, add another sport to your training program. A routine with jogging, bicycling, or swimming helps strengthen your cardiovascular system as well as tone muscles. If you have access to a pool, swimming is particularly good for increasing your heart rate and lung capacity. Also, swimming does not put any extra stress on your joints like jogging does.

Jogging, however, is a convenient form of exercise for those who don't live in a climate where they can swim regularly. Jogging is an inexpensive exercise as long as you run in quality footwear and on even surfaces to reduce the jarring on your ankles and knees. Power walking and long walks in general are also excellent additions to your fitness program, particularly if you have a weak back or knee problems that prohibit you from doing any significant distance running.

Cycling is an excellent form of exercise for increasing leg strength. With the correct seat position, cycling also helps stretch your legs with every downward crank on the pedals.

Always loosen and warm up slowly before any sort of athletic activity, and give yourself a chance to cool down, just as you would your horse. Doing any of these activities at least twice a week, combined with your riding program, can help increase your fitness.

Fitness Exercises

If it's too difficult for you to get out of the house to exercise, you can still get an effective workout with a fitness video, a step routine, or a set of exercises. The most important elements of any exercise program are that you must stick with it, challenge yourself without pushing yourself into an injury, and keep it interesting so that you won't lose your enthusiasm for it.

Here are some exercises that can help you strengthen different areas of your body. They will increase muscle tone, build strength, and develop more suppleness. Be sure to check with your doctor before starting any exercise routine.

First, strengthen your back so that you will reduce the risk of injury as well as improve your range of motion. Because the lower back takes the brunt of the concussion when the horse moves, you should work to build up strength in this area. If you are experiencing recurring back pain, it is wise to make an appointment with an orthopedic specialist, who can diagnose the cause of the pain and recommend treatment.

Next, work on developing your leg muscles. Determine the maximum number of exercise sets that is best for you. Keep in mind that many exercises can be used as stretching exercises before you ride. Also try to concentrate on your breathing, as you want to increase your lung capacity as well as get oxygen to your working muscles.

Plan to start out slowly so that you don't strain any muscle tissue, and then by the second week, increase the repetitions of the exercises. You can design your own program using exercises that you feel are the most beneficial to you. Groups of five to seven different exercises are fine to start out with.

EXERCISE #1   Pelvic Thrust
Lie on the floor with your back flat and your knees bent. Tilt your pelvis up by using your stomach muscles, not your legs. Hold for a count of ten. Do two sets of five daily.

EXERCISE #2   Lateral Trunk Stretch
This exercise should be done slowly. Lie on the floor with your back flat, your arms outstretched, and your legs extended.

Take one of your legs and raise it up with your toe flexed, then swing it over, crossing the other leg, and onto the other side of the floor to rest. Your torso will swing with the leg to improve suppleness. Do two sets of five.

EXERCISE #3   Crunch

Lie on the floor with your back flat and your knees bent, and slowly curl your head and shoulders up and forward. Use your stomach muscles to help you rise. Keep your arms crossed in front of your chest. Do two sets of five.

EXERCISE #4   Calf Stretch

Using a step or a curb, stand on the balls of your feet and slowly lower yourself down 3 inches, allowing your weight to drop into your heels. Then raise yourself back up. Do two sets of ten.

EXERCISE #5   Leg Lift

Lying flat on the floor with the small of your back flat, lift one leg with knee slightly bent upward. Do two sets of ten.

EXERCISE #6   Side Leg Lift

Lie on your side, with the leg closest to the floor bent. Keep your top leg straight, and raise and lower it in two sets of ten.

EXERCISE #7   Side-to-Side Stretch

While standing with a slight bend at the knees, place one hand on your hip and in a slow and smooth motion, stretch over your head with your other arm extended, palm up, and hold for a count of five. Switch hand positions, and stretch over with your other arm. This will help stretch you from the ribcage as well as make you aware of riding faults, such as a "collapsed hip." Do two sets of ten.

Weights

Other exercises will help you increase your strength where you need it most. When you work with free weights, start with a small weight first, such as 2 pounds, and work up to dumbbells that weigh no more than 5 pounds. Do sets of ten vertical arm curls, arm lifts, horizontal chest curls, and

Ways to Save Your Back

BACK BRACE   Many companies are now offering back supports that can be used as a preventative measure if you have a weak or injury-prone back or if you ride often. The back brace generates warmth, so it can add a degree of suppleness while keeping your spine aligned.

THERAPEUTIC SADDLE SEAT PADS   These gel pads are designed to reduce the compression on your spine and distribute your weight evenly. They fit over the saddle's seat to provide you with a comfortable ride. Saddle manufacturers also offer some models that have gel underneath the leather seat of the saddle.

COMFORTABLE PADDOCK BOOTS   When you're not wearing your tall boots to ride, wear paddock boots that have an infusion of athletic footwear technology. Boots such as the Ariat, Miller's Heels Down, or Roper's Horse Shoes can help you both in the saddle and on the ground.

overhead lifts. Do not carry weights or use ankle weights while jogging, as this puts stress on bone and tissue. The ideal way to work with weights is on a weight-training machine, where you can tone a variety of muscle groups in both your legs and arms by using various lifting exercises.

Your exercise program will benefit from days when all you do is stretch. If you have had some time away from riding, or you are not quite as supple as you'd like to be, stretching helps keep your muscles toned and your body flexible. Stretching regularly prevents your muscles from tightening up. Yoga and even martial arts are used by top dressage riders who want to build a general awareness of posture, movement, symmetry, and strength.

Protect your muscles—and particularly your back—in your everyday life. Learn how to lift objects properly. When you have to carry 50-pound bags of feed, don't bend over from your waist to pick them up. Keep your back straight, bend your knees until you are in a squatting position close to the ground, wrap your arms around the bag, pull it toward you, and then stand up.

What to Do About a Lull

Even when you are working diligently, it happens. Your training is going along fine, when suddenly you hit a period with no progression. You find that you are stuck in a rut in which your riding program seems to go into reverse. "I haven't had that problem in months," you tell yourself. "How could this crop back up?"

The same thing can happen with your horse. Without any warning, he may plateau in his ability to do the work you ask. Perhaps an area that you feel has been conquered comes back to haunt you. It could be as subtle as a dull attitude toward his work.

Whether it's your problem or your horse's, you must realize that lulls are natural occurrences in training. Riding is more like a staircase than a trip uphill, with several areas that seem to flatten out before heading upward once again. Simply realizing that it is not unusual to have a lull in progression will enable you to be more positive about getting on with your work again.

Next, step back to evaluate what has been going on. Are you drilling yourself? Are there pressures in your life that are preventing you from concentrating? Are you so engrossed in your riding lessons that you haven't been able to do any type of pleasure riding? Are you not quite 100 percent healthy (perhaps a cold or even a slight sports injury is slowing you down)? These are all things that will affect your performance and your enthusiasm for riding and can contribute to a lull.

If you feel that your horse is causing the lull, he may be subtly resisting you by not giving you his best. He may not be ring-sour, but he may be feeling a bit bored with the work pattern, just going through the motions automatically, without enthusiasm. He might be a little stiff or touchy. He may be fighting off a cold.

If any of these factors are present, take a little time off from dressage and just spend time with your horse. Go on a trail ride, or make time to work with him on the ground, whether you groom, longe, or ground-drive him. Vary his workout patterns and add in turnout or trail time after his workout. If he is truly getting fed up with the game, he needs a little variety in his life, good rewards, and time to be a horse so that he (and in turn you) can get back to being enthusiastic about dressage.

Riding Fears

Anxiety about riding is real and can set you back in subtle or serious ways. Tension or anxiety about getting into the saddle can be transmitted to your horse and can interfere with your success. Some riders only fear certain things: a particular spot in the arena, windy days, a huge canter stride, or an out-of-control horse. Others often build up a subtle fear after a fall or near fall. Some riders who are pushed way too hard by their coaches, to the point that they dread their riding sessions, often blank out stupidly and fear being belittled.

If you suffer from some anxiety about your riding, you're not alone. Realizing that you have a fear is the first step to eliminating it.

Riders communicate fear to horses through body language, and this is counterproductive to riding goals. Some riders tense up and get stiff through the back and seat or become

Tension or fearfulness can be transmitted to your horse and can hamper your success.

rigid in the arms, hands, and legs. Other riders do exactly the opposite by falling apart and allowing too much slack in the reins and too little contact with the horse. Some do a combination of the two. If the horse is easygoing, he may not get all that flustered by the rider's behavior, but if he's sensitive and cannot trust his rider, he will have to act upon instinct. Because horses are prey animals and used to living in herds, their natural instinct for flight could result in shying, running away, balking, or ditching the rider.

To get back into control, many psychologists recommend that you first go to the root of your fear and define it. You may discover that you are afraid of being physically hurt. You may fear being embarrassed by your horse or by your lack of knowledge. After identifying your fear, go to the source of the problem and attempt to discover the cause. Did you have a frightening experience when you fell off your horse and got the wind knocked out of you? Was seeing a friend get seriously injured after a fall all you needed to make you frightened to ride?

If your fear stems from physical pain, you should work to improve your riding and set smaller goals for yourself while working in an area that makes you feel safer. Follow up by watching other successful riders, or read up on dressage to keep expanding your knowledge base. Perhaps listen to a sports psychology audio tape to help you understand how to conquer fear. It's also very important to have an instructor who is supportive of you. She shouldn't coddle you, but neither should she badger you into riding beyond your current capacity. If your horse is scaring you, take a break from him and see if someone else will let you ride a more sedate horse for a while. Riding a mild-mannered mount will help to increase your confidence. Just make arrangements for your horse to get his exercise and regular workouts—perhaps with a friend—so that he will be a nice mount to return to.

You can also build up your self-esteem by logging in as much riding time as possible. Green riders are generally more timid and cautious, even apprehensive. But as the green rider gets more experience—especially positive experience—confidence, as well as the rider's knowledge, can continue to grow. If you believe that you just don't have that much riding experience, yet have the desire to stick it out, you will eventually be able to relax more and ride better.

Set a reasonable goal for your riding so that you can meet it comfortably. It won't do you much good to tell yourself that you must be qualifying your horse for the USDF year-end awards if your horse is not ready. Take, instead, a realistic approach to a goal, and when you are able to accomplish it, you will be that much closer to conquering your fear or anxiety.

Finally, practice mental relaxation techniques such as deep breathing exercises and yoga. Picture in your mind the perfect ride. Think positively about your sessions on horseback, and keep an honest perspective about your riding. Plan for disaster by putting yourself in a solid frame of mind where you can prepare for any type of situation your horse throws your way.

You can help conquer your fear by practicing mental relaxation techniques such as deep-breathing exercises, yoga, and visualizing the perfect ride.

The world won't end if you mess up in a lesson or at a show, and you'll nearly always get another chance to try it again.

If you follow these techniques, you can overcome your fear and anxiety about riding. If you are having severe difficulties, however, talk with a sports psychologist who knows about the unique relationship riders share with their horses.

Your Horse's Physical Changes

When people envision the perfect dressage horse, they picture a sleek, well-muscled horse of grand proportions, floating above the ground at an extended gait with neck arched and haunches driving. In this vision, the horse seems to be doing this without any effort. Unfortunately, this picture doesn't come easily or cheaply; a horse that is fit to do dressage is the result of many months, even years of conditioning and development.

Obviously, a horse that is unfit for the sport has very little muscle on either side of his spine, or his spine sticks out from the topline. A horse that has an underdeveloped neck or a hay belly and is seriously flabby needs to get back into shape before being introduced to any serious work.

Don't rush your horse's conditioning, or you may end up with a severely fatigued or injured horse. Don't stress him by trying to do it all at once. If you have had to take a break from your training because of a long winter, a maternity leave, or a lameness, remember to bring him back gradually so that the lost muscle tone can be developed again.

For your horse to be in condition, determine his fitness by adding up how much time his dressage level requires. For instance, if you ride Training Level, add how much time it takes to warm him up, work him, and then do a four-and-a half-minute test. Then you can work him in three areas: developing his strength, suppleness, and his endurance.

Then, you'll need to know what condition he currently is in by working him for a set period of time and then monitoring his heart rate. Heart-rate monitors are available specifically for horses, and you can place them underneath the girth area to get an accurate reading. However, they are expensive ($150 to $200), so learn how to read his dorsal scapular artery from the saddle by placing the two forefingers of your right hand about 5 inches down the neck and 3 inches in front of the shoulder until you feel his pulse. Get his pulse rate by counting for twenty seconds and multiplying by three. Find out what his normal heart rate is at the walk and then after a work period.

Work him for the set period of time, then measure his heart rate, checking to see how long it takes for his pulse to return to normal. As your workouts progress, your horse's heart rate will return to normal more quickly. This gives you a good picture of what is going on in your horse's body as he gets into shape.

Keep an eye out for troubles when you are working on your horse's fitness. Check for heat, discomfort, or swelling along the ligaments and tendons, cannon bone, and splint bone. Heat in his hooves is also a warning sign of internal inflammation. Use your hands as well as your eyes because they will be able to tell you if there is something that feels a little different. Check any swelling or lumps and bumps against the same area in the other leg. If you find that one is different from the other, your horse probably has an injury.

Pay attention to your horse's behavior because it also tells you a lot about how he is feeling. Observe how much he eats. If he loses his appetite, he may be sick with a virus or be colicky. Keep an eye open to any unusual patterns in his day-to-day life, such as how he reacts to grooming, saddling, pasturemates, etc. Listen as you enter his barn or paddock in the morning and check for any coughs, wheezes, or irregular breathing patterns. If you have any concerns about his health, check his temperature to see if it is elevated. Most healthy horses have a rectal temperature between 98.5 and 101.5° F, but you should know what is normal for your own horse.

Also observe how he reacts from day to day while under saddle. You can pick up on subtle changes in his way of going if you ride him quite a bit in a routine. If you are sticking to the same conditioning program but suddenly find that the horse becomes resistant, for example, in canter transitions, go back and determine how long he's been doing this, what factors made him behave like this, and see if the problem has medical origins, such as a sore back, unfloated teeth, or the like.

Finally, keep him up to date on vaccinations, worming, shoeing, and vet exams. All of these help to keep your horse sound, fit, and working with a good attitude.

Keeping Your Horse's Enthusiasm Up

Horses that are only taken out of their stables to work are prime candidates for becoming sour. The horse that is cooped up in his box stall and only briefly let out for riding sessions will develop a sullen attitude or even stable vices. While you may be very enthusiastic about your riding workload, your horse may think otherwise if he is drilled constantly with no release. Therefore it is crucial to keep him enthusiastic about his work.

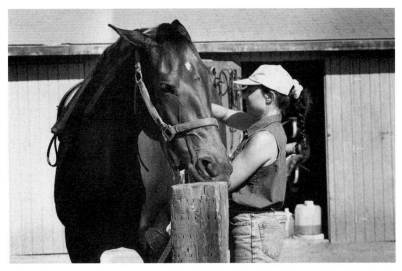

A horse that is grouchy while being groomed or saddled may be souring on his routine, so it is crucial to keep him enthusiastic about his work.

Here are some red flags that let you know your horse is going at his job without joy. He may:

- Act grouchy when groomed or saddled
- Have a dull attitude in the arena
- Refuse to be caught when in pasture
- Show a mild, negative change in temperament

  More serious warning signs include:

- Being reluctant to enter the arena
- Bucking or running away under saddle

- Refusing to eat

- Cribbing, stall-walking, weaving

- Biting and rearing

If you see even mild cases of lackluster attitude, try to build up your horse's overall enthusiasm so that it never gets to be a dangerous or severe situation.

To improve your horse's attitude, make sure that he has adequate turnout time in his week to do as he pleases.

Make sure that your horse has adequate turnout time in his week. Turnout is different from exercise. He should be able to do as he pleases when he is turned out: this is his time. Resist the urge to make him do "something." Many riders think that horses should blow off steam while turned out. Do not go out and chase your horse around a small paddock or crack a longe whip to get him moving. Simply let him be a horse. Make this a regular part of his routine so that he looks forward to having his own version of "free-time." Turnout is more often a mental relaxation than a physical exertion.

When you turn out your horse, walk him prior to setting him loose. In the event that he takes off bucking and jumping down the paddock, he won't strain a tendon or pull a muscle as easily as if he were turned out "cold" from his stall.

If you want to add exercise *on top of* his regular turnout sessions, you can also free-longe your horse by turning him loose in a small paddock or round pen and joining him, but you should stay in the center. This will allow your horse the freedom of moving around on his own, but you will still be there to keep his mind on moving forward in the direction you want.

If you keep your horse on your own property, you probably have access to pasture or paddock, so your horse will not be captive in his stall all day long. But even long hours of turnout can be detrimental if the horse does not have adequate shade from the summer sun or shelter from the wind in the winter. If you turn your horse out for several hours at a time during fly season, you may want to put a fly mask on him and spray him with repellent to make his time out more comfortable. Also, if your horse is turned out in a dry lot with no grass to nibble, you may want to give him low-protein hay in a ground feeder to allow him the mental relaxation of grazing. In cold winter months, provide him with protection from the elements, such as a run-in shelter.

As far as your riding goes, vary your program. Horses are creatures of habit, but they will get bored if they don't have variety within their routine. If you have access to different arenas, use them all so that your horse doesn't get used to always working in the same one. If you only have one ring at home, see if there is a neighbor who wouldn't mind sharing arenas with you. Your horse will benefit from being exposed to new locations. If there is no other arena to ride in, you can still vary your routine by having extended walk-tours around the property before you begin your work or after you have finished.

If your horse was ridden in a different discipline (or has talent for more than one), let him do both occasionally to break up the monotony. After his dressage workout, pop him over a couple of fences if he likes to jump. If he enjoys trails, reward him with a leisurely stroll after your serious schooling. Practice things like going over bridges, through gates and water, and over ground poles.

Work with your horse on ground manners by picking up his feet or clipping him. You can also practice carrot stretches, having him reach around for a carrot in a variety of ways to help stretch neck and topline muscles, to keep him supple and interested in what you are doing. If you don't have access to pasture, but do have a spot for grazing, take him on a long lead and let him spend an hour eating grass.

New Ways to Make the Work Fun

- Find a friend that you can ride a *pas de deux* with.

- Use a cassette player and headphones so you can ride to music. If you buy one of those new saddle pads that have speakers in them, you don't have to wear a headset.

Help yourself stay out of ruts by finding a friend you can practice a pas de deux with.

(continues)

Use a cassette player and headphones so you can ride to music.

- Take turns with a friend videotaping your schooling sessions, and then watch the tapes.

- Have a friend shoot still photography of you so you can evaluate your position later.

- Organize educational video parties with like-minded dressage friends.

- Hold impromptu "shows" with a couple of other riders. Take turns being the judge so that everybody gets a chance to critique each other's performance.

- Hold gymkhana events with other riders where the objective is to improve your horsemanship and have fun. Take events that are normally based on speed, such as pole bending or an egg-and-spoon race, and emphasize accuracy to help improve your aids. Other games on horseback, such as follow-the-leader and ride-a-buck (where the rider keeps a dollar in place under the thigh at various gaits), will help your equitation as well as your balance on the horse, and you'll probably feel great about using your horse for a fun event instead of work.

Ways to Stay Out of Schooling Ruts

- Incorporate new ways to teach yourself by designing a lesson plan for your schooling session. Otherwise, a ride without a plan usually turns out to be exactly like the one you had the day before. Make a special riding calendar, and list the objectives that you'd like to accomplish. Then write down how you would like to accomplish them.

- Ride with a friend and try to keep side by side or in tandem, maintaining a predetermined distance throughout the entire session.

To maintain your horse's level of enthusiasm, always end on a good note. Reward him with a pat and walk him out of his training arena.

(continues)

- Set your watch and ride in timed segments. When your time is up, put your horse on a long rein for a couple of minutes to give him a break.

- After completing most of your work, let him go at a nice, easy hand-gallop pace to clear out the lungs and mind.

- Ride your practice sessions without stirrups or with just a bareback pad.

- Take a dressage test that is not familiar to you into the ring and have a go at it.

- End on a positive note and immediately leave the arena.

- Go for a cool-down walk, or dismount and hand-walk your good horse.

Chapter Seven

Other Training Methods

*Y*our lessons are progressing smoothly. You feel as though you are getting a lot of information and value out of them. But what about learning from someone other than your instructor? You've heard about well-known riders who give special clinics for novices. Are these also of value?

The answer to that is generally yes. Riding with a different, often more-experienced teacher can give you an entirely new picture of your current riding ability. Some clinicians may come from other parts of the country, or even other countries, and therefore will offer a unique perspective. In a riding clinic, you get an evaluation of your horse's progress, too.

Not all clinics are equal, however. Choose a clinic with your current instructor's help. Even though famous riders or trainers give clinics regularly, not all of them are able to effectively communicate their methods to the public. Worse, there may be a few "bad apples" whose methods you may question, and when you are stuck in a clinic with them, you are at their mercy for at least an hour. The less desirable clinicians may do something to your horse that could take a lot of undoing when you get home, so research the instructor well before signing up.

Find out about training clinics in your area through postings at your local tack shop, the local or state dressage chapter newsletter, or the free horse newspapers around your region.

Find out about training clinics in your area through postings at your local tack shop, the newsletter of your local or state dressage chapter, or the free horse newspapers in your vicinity. Most clinics are held at large equestrian facilities, so be sure to inquire about any events on their schedules. Some clinicians will post fliers at neighboring facilities, in hope that riders will come from all around the area.

Some clinicians are well-known riders who ride at FEI level. Some are judges who can give you insight into your riding from their unique perspective. Some are USDF-certified instructors who, having passed their rigorous training program, can communicate what they learned from that program. Others are local trainers who have developed a solid reputation and have successful horses and students under their tutelage. Try to find other riders who have already ridden with the clinician and determine if the session would be a good opportunity for you.

If you feel ready to try a dressage clinic, it is fairly easy to sign up and participate, and the experience is well worth it. Make sure that you have your spot reserved and that you know what time you are to ride. Also, be certain that the clinic is for riders like yourself so that you will not be wasting your time or the clinician's by showing up at a Fourth Level clinic when you only ride Training Level.

You may want to watch a clinic take place before you actually sign up to ride in one. Because of the costs involved in attending a clinic, you can educate yourself by observing a clinic first.

What to Expect

You should plan to work hard. Clinics range in price and intensity, but generally, you should be prepared to ride for at least forty-five minutes, with perhaps a couple of two-minute breaks that will let you catch your breath and allow the clinician to evaluate your progress for the session. Some clinics are very reasonable—not much more than a regular private lesson—while others can soar into triple digits. What you get out of it is what you put into it.

You should be fit enough to ride for the duration of the clinic, as you will be wasting your time if you are exhausted after a ten-minute warm-up. Your horse should also be fit enough to perform some serious work. Your horse doesn't have to be able to do every movement that is requested, but if you want to do work at a particular level, your horse should at least have the capability of attaining some of that level's goals within the session.

Prepare yourself for a different type of schooling. Some clinicians get quite animated when they are trying to express ideas, and some riders may interpret this as anger or agitation. Perhaps some clinicians do get angry when they see a rider not responding to their instruction. Be aware that there are many styles of teaching and that some teachers may yell if they don't get the immediate response they are after. Likewise, some are very encouraging and will praise any effort made. It is best to go into the arena with an open mind and focus on your riding at all times. Usually a teacher will not berate you, but if you take any little criticism as, "Oh, this person HATES me," you need to get a thicker skin before you sign up for a clinic.

Additionally, the clinician may want to ride your horse, so be prepared to let him or her mount up. If you have any reservations about having your horse ridden, let the clinic organizer know well beforehand. Some clinics offer group lessons. If this is the case, you should be prepared to participate with a number of horses. Your horse should be able to work with other horses without being naughty or disruptive. You should also be able to keep him at the same pace as the other pupils' horses so that you are not always rushing past or catching up to the rest of the group.

What the Teacher Expects

The clinician is on a tight schedule and usually has several horses and riders to evaluate and instruct throughout the day. Therefore, be prepared to go at the precise time you are scheduled, with your horse warmed up and wearing appropriate, well-adjusted tack. If one of the rides before you is running a little late, keep your horse walking and stay close by the arena so you can promptly enter after the other horse finishes. You can also stake out a friend at the gate and have her get you if you would like to use that extra time in the warm-up ring.

Save your questions for logical breaks during your clinic session.

The clinician expects your full attention. He or she also expects courtesy and obedience. Now is not the time to tell the clinician, "That's not how I was taught," or, "I prefer to execute it this way." You should raise questions only at a break in the ride, unless you absolutely cannot follow the instruction. You should be able to concentrate and respond to instruction. Sometimes you may be working on one aspect of your riding, for instance, keeping an outside leg back with weight in the heel, and you may forget that you've collapsed a hip in the process. However, you should at least make an attempt to execute the commands of the instructor so that he or she can see the progress being made.

A Typical Clinic

Clinics vary according to the instructor, but they are usually intense and inspiring, and they give you insight into what your riding is like up to this point.

Your horse should be wearing clean, well-fitting tack because the clinician will often inspect your tack before you even begin. You should make certain it is presentable.

Treat the clinic day like a show day; be prepared to do your best and learn. Plan ahead, and make sure that you have everything you need. Both you and your horse should be properly turned out for a clinic. He should wear clean, well-fitting tack (the clinician will often inspect the fit of your tack before you even begin, so make certain that it is present-able). Most clinicians will want your horse's legs protected, so he should be wearing polo wraps, tendon boots, or sports medicine boots that are properly applied. He should be clean and well-groomed, meaning a freshly trimmed bridlepath, no shavings in his tail, no mud in his coat, and no dirt in his nose.

You should wear tall boots and breeches. Your shirt should be a close-fitting top, such as a polo shirt or a riding blouse. Billowy shirts prevent the clinician from seeing your riding form, and he or she won't be able to tell if you've hollowed your back, collapsed a hip, or hunched your shoulders. If you are going to be out in the sun, wear light colors so you don't get overheated. Many clinicians recommend that their pupils wear helmets for safety as well. Bring gloves, spurs (optional), and a dressage whip.

If you have to trailer to the clinic, leave yourself plenty of time to unload, settle your horse, tack up, and warm up. Depending upon your ride time, two hours before will usually be adequate. You may want to check in with the organizer and perhaps watch a prior ride to get a feel for what lies ahead for you.

Put on your horse's saddle and bridle, and double-check for proper fit. Mount up, and let your horse walk around to stretch out. This also allows him time to get used to the new surroundings. Let him stretch out at the walk for several minutes before pushing him into your solid warm-up.

Unlike at a show, there will not be as many riders warming up at the same time as you are because the rides are staggered throughout the day. However, be courteous to the regular riders and boarders at the equestrian facility. There may be other lessons going on with different trainers, so try to be as considerate as possible in the warm-up arena. Ask if there is a particular area you should stay out of, such as jumping courses or longeing circles.

A twenty-minute warm-up is probably all you will need before entering the arena for your lesson. Get your horse loose, relaxed, and moving forward off of your leg. Any difficulties that you believe may hinder your lesson should be worked out beforehand, such as lack of suppleness, inattention to your aids, rushing, etc. If your horse is nervous about being away from home, don't worry: most clinicians will understand and work to relax you and your horse with a set of exercises.

Your Lesson

You will probably be asked for some information about your riding experience and your horse's background. You will then be asked to ride for about five minutes, while the clinician evaluates you. He or she will ask you to halt, give you a short evaluation, and perhaps follow up with some questions about your riding goals. The rest of the clinic will be focused on helping you move toward achieving those goals.

Clinics provide you with a great deal of information, so don't feel as though you must remember every detail. If you want to catch every moment of the ride, it is wise to have your session videotaped. Reviewing a videotape of your session with someone other than your regular teacher will not only provide you with feedback on your clinic lesson, but your success at the clinic can also show you how your regular lessons have paid off. Check first with the clinic manager to see if it is okay to videotape.

Save your questions for logical breaks during the ride. Often the clinician will ask you for your input. However, make this session a time for taking in information, not a discourse on how you feel your own riding is coming along.

Although most clinic sessions are short (under an hour), they ask a lot of you and your horse. They are, however, very uplifting and will often leave you with the feeling of "empowered" riding—like you have just conquered a mountain. After a positive experience at a clinic, you can take home the information gleaned and put it to use in your regular riding sessions.

Premature Ending

If you believe that the clinician is asking more than you can give, or if you or your horse are truly in too poor of shape to continue the lesson, or if you have been instructed to punish your horse beyond what you feel is correction, you may choose to end your session voluntarily. Do so in a professional manner with as much discretion as possible. Try not to get angry or upset. Merely tell the person that you are unable to continue with the lesson and are asking permission to withdraw. If you feel that the clinician is taking it too person-ally and becomes agitated, you may dismount, exit the arena, and explain the reasons for your withdrawal to the event orga-nizer. You must stand up for yourself or your horse if the clinic gets to be too much for you. If a clinic turns out other than you expected, just consider it an experience, and don't feel that all clinics are like that. Most are genuinely uplifting.

Bring the Clinic to You

It's not difficult to set up a clinic at your own boarding facil-ity. First, contact your stable management and get permission to hold such an event. Certain insurance issues will need to be addressed, and management will undoubtedly want to benefit monetarily for the use of their arena for the day. Then, talk with other interested riders and get a solid head count of all the people who would want to participate. Next, contact your state dressage chapter for a list of trainers or judges, or get a list of their clinicians. Call and interview clinicians until you find one who you enjoy talking with and who gives clinics to riders at the level of those who will attend. Let the clinician know how many people will come, and try to set up a day that works best for all concerned.

You may have to follow up to make sure that those who expressed interest in participating actually pay and show up for their session, but having a clinic at your horse's home will be well worth the trouble. Open the clinic up to more than just your stable by posting fliers at the local tack shops. This way, riders even in the more remote areas will help fill your clini-cian's roster.

Audit a Clinic

You can benefit from attending, rather than participating in, a clinic given by a major name in the dressage world: a renowned judge, a grand prix rider, or a famous trainer. This is called auditing. When you audit, you are able to sit in on a clinic, take notes, occasionally ask questions, watch, and learn. Auditing a clinic can give you insight into different aspects of dressage, for example, longeing the horse or learning how dressage is judged.

As an auditor, you will pay a fraction of what the participants will pay. You don't have to feel that being a novice is a detriment either, because you can learn a good deal by just watching. Talk to the organizer about what the day's events will cover and this will help you determine how to use the clinic to your best advantage.

It's good to bring a chair, a hat, and a notebook or tape recorder (or video recorder). You may want to bring your own lunch with you too, just in case they do not have any food at the facility. Sharing the day with a friend can be a good way to evaluate the program after the day has ended.

Other Learning Opportunities

There are other ways to increase your knowledge of dressage and educate yourself on a different aspect of the sport.

Scribes, Scorers, and Volunteer Work

One of the best ways to learn about dressage is from a judge, and the best way you can spend time with a judge is to be a scribe. A scribe sits next to the judge during a competition and writes down the judge's scores of a dressage test. This is done so the judge never has to take her eyes off the competitor. As each rider is evaluated, the judge will often give comments for the scribe to record. Therefore, a scribe can gain a good understanding of what the judge is looking for and why she is scoring the way she is. It is almost like having television commentary for every test.

When the judge gives her score in numerical points, she will usually follow it with her review of that movement. You

To learn more about dressage, volunteer to work as a scribe. A scribe writes down the judge's scores of a dressage test. This is done so that the judge never has to take her eyes off the competitor.

may see a pattern in what the judge is looking for, and this can help you with your own riding. If the judge continually looks for relaxation and suppleness in the horses and finds one horse that is super, make a mental note of what the duo looks like for your own riding knowledge.

However, it's important to remember that if you get the opportunity to scribe, you are there to work, and learning is just the byproduct of your experience. If you get carried away and sit in the judge's booth just watching the test, you will probably incur the wrath of every rider who receives a blank comment box on their test. The judge will also have your head, because when she reviews the test prior to signing it, she will have to go back and tell you her comments again for you to write down.

Volunteer to be a scribe by contacting your local dressage chapter or show organizers and letting them know that you're available, trustworthy, have good penmanship, and are very flexible. Schooling shows are always in need of volunteers and are a good place for you to learn without the pressure of rated shows.

If you take a volunteer position as a scorer, you will be in charge of adding up the rider's test points and determining the percentage score for the ride. You may not get to see much of the show, depending on where tests are added up, but you will get to see how tests are scored, what the judge looks for, and how a show operates.

Another volunteer position that can help you learn about dressage is the test runner, the person who takes the completed tests from the scribe to the scorer. You can also volunteer to be at the in-gate or assist the show secretary. No matter what your role is at a show, you will be invaluable to the workings of the event, and the experience will be invaluable.

USDF Adult Dressage Camps

Most people have such positive experiences at a clinic that they don't want the day to end. If a one-day clinic seems too short for you, dressage camp should be right for you. Intensive schooling and theory are the name of the game here, and adult riders of all skill levels and experience come together to learn and to meet new compatriots. Well-known instructors and trainers often head the riding sessions. Camps also offer supplementary learning sessions that will help you improve your horse and your mental outlook on riding. The groups are usually small (under twenty participants).

USDF Adult Dressage Camps have been available since 1993. Recently there have been more opportunities to participate in these camps, which are now being held throughout the United States. The camps usually run from two to five days, with participants riding twice a day. Camps also supplement the riding sessions with seminars, demonstrations, lectures, and videos.

Conventions

If you want to get involved in the inner workings of the USDF, or plan on becoming seriously involved in showing, the USDF's annual convention is part business, part pleasure, and almost everyone who attends comes back with positive comments. The convention allows attendees to see first-hand what is happening in the sport, as well as participate in the organization that is shaping dressage on national and local levels.

Regions and the Board of Governors hold a series of meetings at the convention. Various committees and councils function throughout the year in an advisory capacity, and their reports help keep the USDF informed of things that are important on a regional level. AHSA rule changes are also discussed in many of the sessions. A host of seminars review current topics important to the organization, such as the instructor certification program, the judging programs, regional championships, and awards.

The USDF also has sessions called USDF University, in which well-known individuals in the industry focus on such topics as riding fundamentals and the mental aspects of the sport. Some sessions concentrate on the showing aspect of the tests, but others can help with your day-to-day riding and instruction.

Symposiums

Attending a symposium offers you a wonderful learning experience and the chance to meet other dressage enthusiasts, including renowned national and international trainers and judges. Important topics in the sport are always on the agenda. You will find that symposiums are more than demonstrations, as many allow time for helpful question-and-answer sessions. They are extremely interactive, and they allow you to expand your knowledge on many levels. Seating is often limited, so you must register early.

Not all symposiums are related to dressage, however. Lectures given by trainers who work with problem horses, such as the renowned John Lyons, Richard Shrake, and Dennis Reis, can be fascinating to attend. Symposiums on The TTouch Method®, devised by Linda Tellington-Jones, can also provide excellent insight into helping your horse reach his potential by eliminating pain and fear from his routine. Symposiums on nutrition, rider fitness, equine sports medicine, and veterinary breakthroughs are all good topics that make riders into knowledgeable horsemen and horsewomen.

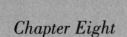

Chapter Eight

Preparing for Your First Show

$\mathcal{N}$ow that you have been schooling in dressage for some time, you may want to check your progress by way of a competition. This is your opportunity to measure all that you've learned over the previous months. If you've shown in other disciplines before, you may have already enjoyed the excitement and competitive nature of horse shows. But dressage shows are slightly different from hunter/jumper, saddleseat, or western shows.

First, you will be in the ring by yourself, not with a host of other riders. The judge watches your entire ride and stays focused on you while his or her comments are written down by a scribe. You will get written feedback, which takes all the guesswork out of what the judge thought of your test. You will probably ride in only two classes for the day, as opposed to the typical four to six most riders enter at other types of shows. Because your ride times will more than likely be close together, you don't need to show up at the show grounds at the crack of dawn and stay there until sunset.

Your schooling and practice sessions at home should be solid enough so that when you show, you should be able to compete without any serious difficulties. You should feel confident that you are executing material that is second nature, rather than elements you are just beginning to work on in lessons. Many instructors suggest that their riders show at a level lower than the one they are schooling at so they can be as relaxed and comfortable as possible with the test requirements. Since factors such as trailering, unfamiliar show-grounds, different footing, and various barn noises—not to mention typical show-day jitters—will affect your performance, it is better to play it safe and ride a test that you have confidence executing.

Check out the opportunities in your area to participate in a small dressage show.

Choosing a Test

The USDF and AHSA work in tandem to create riding tests that challenge the rider-and-horse team at the current level in which they show. Each level has its own aims or "objectives" to help further the goals of dressage. While Training Level is America's first widely-recognized test category for the novice, there is also a division called Introductory, which is the most basic. Intro Tests 1 and 2 are also referred to as USDF Walk/Trot classes, as there is no canter work. The tests are designed to ease beginning riders into the process of riding tests and provide the novice dressage rider with a way to become exposed to dressage protocol.

Introductory tests give new riders a good opportunity to demonstrate some basic skills. Because all of the trot work is ridden rising, it allows the rider to concentrate on making correct, quality movements. Since the objectives are to make smooth transitions, the rider can also sit the trot when going from trot to walk. At Introductory Level, the judge wants to see the horse ridden on a light but steady contact. The judge places more importance on how the rider prepares the horse for each movement and makes the movement high-quality and correct rather than on the horse's gaits or his executing the movement exactly at the specified marker. As you peruse the tests, you'll notice there are many movements that can be made between two markers, allowing the rider a wide margin in which to execute the required movement.

Training-Level tests place emphasis on a supple and free-moving horse that wants to go forward in a clear and steady rhythm while accepting contact with the bit at the walk, trot, and canter. The horse is asked to perform 20-meter circles and serpentines, along with a 10-meter half-circle to turn onto centerline. These movements are not difficult in themselves, but they do require the rider to show straightness on the centerline, quality in the turns, calm and smooth canter departs, quality in the horse's transitions and gaits, correct and round circles and serpentines, and balance throughout the test.

Learning your test is not that difficult, particularly at the lowest levels. Introductory- and Training-Level tests are short, and the movements are basic, so approach it as you would memorize a speech or directions to someone's house. If you find that you get lost, or that the movements are confusing, break the test down into sections when memorizing it.

At home, have a friend listen to you as you recite the test out loud. According to sports psychologists who use visualization techniques, verbalizing the test not only promotes better memorization, but it also makes the movement more tangible and solidifies the element in your subconscious. It may help you to draw the test on a piece of rectangular paper. Some riders like to practice memorizing the test on foot, imitating the horse's gaits in a mini "arena."

Concentrate on the quality of the movement as well as the execution of the movement. Don't drill your horse too much when practicing the tests. Repetition not only kills your horse's enthusiasm, it can also make him anticipate the movements and execute transitions before you ask for them. During your practice, if you have had a few successful trial runs for the day, end the session on a good note to keep him fresh. For instance, if your horse is making a correct 10-meter half-circle and ending up right on centerline at least three times, you can stop asking for that movement and move on to something else, or quit for the day. You could also try riding completely different patterns from the tests you have been riding. If you are planning to ride more than one test, try to ride the tests back to back and then in a different order so that your horse doesn't anticipate your cues.

Choosing Your Show

Your instructor will help you determine when you are ready to compete at a show. Your first show should probably be a schooling show, instead of a recognized show, for more than one reason. Recognized, or rated, shows often count toward state or regional qualifications, and therefore the competition is stiffer and the entry fees are higher. Schooling shows are ideal for the first time out because organizers are a little more lenient on rider dress and protocol, and the judges are more generous with constructive criticism and encouragement.

Ask your instructor to help you determine the most suitable show for you to attend.

Schooling shows are a good place to start, and a good portion of the competitors will also be performing the USDF Introductory-Level and Training-Level tests.

Rarely do you see riders beyond Second Level at a schooling show, so you'll be in good company. You'll see plenty of different riding styles and equine breeds as well. There is a nice camaraderie at schooling shows, and often you'll see the same faces competing at the different local shows.

When you and your instructor have selected your show, call for a prize list, and when you receive it, read it over carefully. There may be some details that are unique to that particular show. Mail your entry fee and form in before the due date noted on the prize list. This protocol is different from most open western and hunter shows, where you can just trailer in early and sign up in the show office that morning. Since ride times are always assigned, the show management must receive all entries in order to schedule rides and contact riders. The exception to this is that when a rider scratches from the competition, that time slot becomes available. When there is an empty time slot, a late entry can sign up on show day and ride in that slot.

When the show management receives all entries, they will either contact you by telephone or by mail with your ride times. However, it is your responsibility to find out your ride times if you do not hear from the show management. On the chance that the organizers or management were unable to get in touch with you, call the office two days before the show to get your times. If you want to receive your ride times by mail, enclose a self-addressed, stamped envelope with your entry.

You may have to show evidence that your horse has had a negative Coggins test before your entry can be accepted. A Coggins test is a U.S. Department of Agriculture–approved blood test that determines whether a horse has Equine Infectious Anemia. This often deadly disease is spread by biting insects that transmit the disease from one horse to another. Depending upon its severity, it is a painful disease for which there is no vaccination and no cure, so the only way to prevent it from spreading from horse to horse is to isolate infected horses. To obtain a certificate for a negative Coggins test, a veterinarian must take a blood sample and send it to an authorized lab that will test the blood. A Coggins test may be required for "admission" to a show, depending on your state laws and the size of the show.

It is also up to you to let show management know if you have any special requirements on show day or, if it is a multi-day show, what your stabling needs are. Let show management know if you are going to be trailering in with another rider so that your ride times can be arranged near each other. If you do have scheduling conflicts, call the show secretary immediately.

Because of the amount of preparation you'll be doing, including memorization and warm-up, your best bet is to enter only two classes. For instance, if you are showing Introductory Level 1 and 2 (the Walk/Trot tests), it is enough for the day to concentrate on learning those patterns and making them the best you can.

There are few riders who like to enter three classes, treating the first class as a warm-up and the other two as the real thing. They want to give their horse a chance to look at everything in the arena so that if they come unglued in the first test, they still have the opportunity to come back and relax for the other two. How many classes you enter is up to you, but with an effective warm-up and practice and experience behind you, you might never have to deal with a horse that spooks at everything the first time around, and you can ride both your tests with confidence.

Another reason to ride a maximum of two tests is the extensive physical and mental conditioning that accompanies each ride. Unlike a hunter show, where riders generally warm up over fences and then wait an hour until it is their turn to go into the ring, dressage riders want to make sure that the elements they worked on in the warm-up are transferred to their test. They generally ride right from the warm-up arena to the dressage arena. Also, you will be working on elements that take a great deal of mental and physical energy from a horse-and-rider team that is just starting out. It is not wise to expect your horse to perform three tests. If you ride him until he's got nothing left, he may become sour and uncooperative in the future.

Dressage classes range in price from about fifteen dollars at small schooling shows to about thirty-five dollars at state-rated shows. As with any other show, there are grounds fees and drug fees, so a show day can cost you anywhere from forty dollars to eighty dollars. Shows that are recognized by state dressage chapters, the AHSA, and the USDF (known as "triple-rated" shows) can cost even more per class and have a host of other membership fees added.

Ribbons are awarded at dressage shows in the same fashion as hunter and western shows. Ribbons are usually awarded through fifth or sixth place. Some will have an extra award for first place, ranging from grooming items at schooling shows to wine glasses and crystal at rated shows. Most dressage riders believe that taking home a ribbon is secondary to bettering their previous dressage score, because they are not necessarily competing against anyone but themselves.

Outfitting Yourself

The basic attire that you are required to wear at a schooling show is usually boots, breeches, a light-colored shirt, and a hunt cap or helmet. However, you should check with the show management (if it is not stated on the prize list) to determine what the show's unique requirements are. For instance, most schooling shows will note on the prize list whether jackets are optional. In general, any hunt-seat clothing is considered appropriate. At a schooling show, you can feel quite comfortable in a pair of light breeches, tall English boots, white shirt (preferably ratcatcher style, with a choker), and a dark hunt coat.

However, as you progress, you will feel more confident and correct in the arena in dressage apparel. Even at small rated shows and at the lower levels, many riders wear formal dressage attire, and while judges are not supposed to weigh your apparel in with your appearance, you do want to look your best when riding in this sport. It shows that you are serious and committed, and that you respect the sport's traditions. So outfit yourself appropriately and you'll feel more confident about your ride.

Dressage coats feature a single vent in the back and fit a little looser than a traditional "equitation style" hunt coat. There are four buttons up the front and they are traditionally black, or in some cases, navy blue.

The dressage show coat is usually wool or a wool blend, although polyester is also used. During the warmer months of the show season, it can get pretty hot wearing wool (which is a far cry from the origins of riding apparel in Europe's chilly climate), so "tropical" wool fabrics have been introduced to keep the rider cooler.

Dressage coats have a single vent in the back and four buttons in the front, and fit a little looser than a traditional "equitation style" hunt coat. Coats are traditionally black, although navy is also worn.

Buy a coat that fits well through the shoulders and permits movement in the arms and through the back. It should be cut longer than a hunt coat, and the sleeves should be long enough to cover your wrists with your arms in the riding position. When trying on coats, see if you can get a folding chair in front of a mirror and straddle it as you would a horse, then put yourself in riding position. This will give you a good idea of how the coat would fit you in the saddle. An even better test, if the store permits, is to sit in a dressage saddle.

Dressage breeches—usually white—can be close fitting or have a pleated front, with a regular or high waist. Leather full-seat breeches are popular with dressage riders because they allow a more secure feel in the saddle.

Dressage breeches are usually white, although cream-colored breeches are sometimes in vogue. Breeches can either be close fitting or pleated in front, with a regular or high waist. Leather full-seat breeches are a true luxury, but many dressage riders insist on them because they allow them to have a more secure feel in the saddle. If you opt for cream breeches, you should carry this color throughout, with a cream-colored saddle pad, shirt, and stock tie.

Breeches come in a variety of fabrics. Nylon used to be the most widely available fabric, but while nylon wears like iron, it does not breathe well. Newer cotton blends and synthetic blends are lighter weight and many wick away moisture.

Buy white breeches a little looser than you normally would a regular pair, as white tends to get a little "see-through" when they are tight. Women can also purchase riding underwear that is designed to reduce panty lines. If you are splurging for full-seat breeches, make sure that you have ridden in them before the show date, because they will give you a different feeling in the saddle and possibly affect your riding.

Any collarless English riding shirt will suffice. Do not wear a collared shirt, because dressage riders wear a stock tie. Your shirt can be long- or short-sleeved. If you do decide to get a sleeveless shirt to wear under your jacket on a hot show day, take along a short- or long-sleeved shirt, just in case the judge has all riders remove coats. According to AHSA rules, sleeveless shirts worn without a jacket are not allowed at any rated show.

Shirts come in a variety of fabrics as well: Cotton tends to breathe the best, but it wrinkles more than a cotton/poly blend. Polyester shirts get sticky under a warm coat, but they are affordable and don't wrinkle. Decide what fits your body and budget best.

Stock ties give the whole dressage outfit an elegant, traditional look. Stock ties can be made of various materials (silk, satin, cotton, and blends), and they come pre-tied as a dickey,

Choose a collarless English riding shirt, with either long or short sleeves, to wear with your stock tie.

or untied. If you are a purist, you will want to tie the stock yourself, but if you think you are going to be all thumbs on show morning, it is better to get a pre-tied stock.

Gloves are a matter of taste. Black leather gloves are a safe and conservative choice, as are gloves that feature a leather grip and a stretch fabric over the top of the hand. White gloves are seen on many dressage riders, and they look very elegant, but remember that white draws attention to the hands. Unless your own hands are very steady and quiet, save the white gloves for the upper levels.

If you have been riding in paddock boots or riding sneakers, it is time to invest in tall boots. There are two styles available for English riders: dress and field style. The field style, which has lacing at the foot, is more appropriate for hunt-seat than dressage, so choose dress boots whenever possible. There are rubber or PVC boots for the budget-minded who don't want to spend more than about fifty dollars; leather dress boots start at around one hundred dollars. Stock boots in regular sizes can be bought at tack shops or through catalogs and are generally less expensive than custom, made-to-order boots.

How to Tie a Stock Tie

It's just a square knot. Or is it? Tying a stock frustrates many riders, but if you practice in front of a mirror, re-tying it several times, it will become second nature to you. If your tie has a buttonhole, fasten the stock to the top button on your rat-catcher and cross the tie at the back of your neck, bringing the ends around to the front. If your tie has a slot or opening, place the opening of the tie at the back of your neck and bring the longer end through the opening. Pull the end right around to the front of your neck.

Cross the right end over the left (keeping the left straight), and fold the right underneath the left. Bring the right up and through so that you have half of your knot.

Then make a loop with the right end (which will be on the top half of the knot), and . . .

. . . pull the left end through the right.

Now your knot is complete, but your stock still isn't. Straighten out your knot so that it lies flat, and then take each side of the tie and pull the wrinkles out of it as well.

Cross the right side of the tie over with the left, fluffing out the tie's sides. Then secure it to your ratcatcher with your stock pin at the base of your neck.

A dress boot that is designed especially for dressage differs slightly from the dress boot for hunt-seat riders. It has a stiffer shaft and will often be double lined with leather all the way down the shaft to fully support the rider's leg and to resist wrinkles. Hunt-seat dress boots have a very tall shaft, as is the style, and are often just reinforced at the cuff with a lining. When they break in, they drop down at the ankle into many folds. Dressage riders do not want the folds, but instead opt for more support at the ankle. Stiffer boots, however, can be much more painful during the break-in period, and because of the double leather and the type of leather used, they are often the most expensive type of boot you can buy. Boots that feature Spanish tops curve slightly at the top of the shaft, unlike regular boots, which are cut straight across the top. This cut is more flattering to the leg and is a popular style.

If you are buying dress boots, they should fit as close to your calf and foot as possible. They should be tall enough so that when they do break in and drop down slightly, they will still touch the back of your knee. If you find that they are too difficult to get on and off even with the help of boot pulls and a jack, have a professional put in zippers along the back or short gussets along the inside of the shaft. Both will be relatively inconspicuous and allow you to get in and out of the boots with ease.

Finally, your headgear should either be a hunt cap or a derby. Most American riders at the lower levels wear hunt caps, as derbies are not often available at local tack shops.

A black velvet riding helmet with a harness that is ASTM/SEI–safety approved is required for riders eighteen years of age or under, and completely appropriate and recommended for adults. You will see these helmets on more and more competitors as the "stigma" of wearing safety gear disappears. Safety helmets are designed to be correct for the show ring and are also made to save your head from impact, while a regular hunt cap or derby will not.

What the Stylish Dressage Rider Wears

- Leather full-seat breeches, high-waisted or pleated front

- Stock tie (never a bib or pre-tied stock) with gold stock pin

- White 100-percent-cotton long-sleeved shirt

- Black medium-weight wool coat with waist seam and flared back

- Black leather gloves

- Comfortable sport undergarments and sport socks

- ASTM/SEI helmet

- Show-bow for longer hair

- Fully lined, Spanish-top dress boots

- Small earrings and conservative makeup

- A winning smile

Preparation for the Show

Once you have entered and have your attire together, it is time to get organized. Prepare your horse and yourself by using show checklists (see pages 168 through 170), because lists eliminate the worry of forgetting an item. If you check everything off on paper as you pack, you will sleep better the night before the show.

You need to clip your horse, pull his mane and/or tail, bathe him, braid his mane, and clean his tack. If you choose, you can bathe and clip your horse the day before the show, but with your last practice session, tack cleaning, and braiding, it can make for a very long day for you and your horse. Also, bathing your horse may strip his coat of the essential oils that make the hair shine and lay down smoothly. If you give your horse a bath a couple of days before the show, you can work the natural oils back up to the skin's surface through grooming. Not having to bathe your horse the day before will also free up your pre-show schedule. Schedule your last practice session at an hour that will allow you ample time to braid your horse and pack for the show without rushing. Your last serious schooling session with your instructor should actually happen a few days before your show. It should include several mock tests. Ride as you would in a real test. Don't do anything that you wouldn't do in the real test. For instance, if your instructor tells you that you are off course, correct yourself, continue with the movement, and finish the test, rather than starting over. If you usually counterflex your horse to get him straight on your circles, work on more of a subtle bend, as that is an element you will be scored on. Do not speak to your horse during mock tests.

If you don't normally train in an arena with letters, this is one day to get out your markers so that your "geometry" is more accurate. Always ask your instructor for a silent "judged round" and then get a critique at the end.

One aspect of showing that riders often overlook but shouldn't is the salute. Since each test (with the exception of the USDF Introductory tests) begins and ends with a salute, it is a movement that can really set the tone for your entire ride.

Practice your halting and saluting. When you come to a complete halt, hold both reins and your whip in one hand and drop your free arm down at your side, and then nod your head smartly. You don't have to bow your head as if you're going to be knighted, nor do you have to give yourself whiplash by snapping back up military-style. Pick up your reins after your nod and get yourself situated. This movement doesn't have to be performed at rapid speed, either. You will have time to get

Before the show, practice the halt and salute. Come to a complete halt, putting reins and whip in one hand. Dropping your free arm at your side, nod your head smartly.

an even contact on the reins, alert your horse that he will be moving off, and give him his cue to move forward.

Once you include a nice, smart-looking salute in your repertoire, any judge will take notice that you pay attention to detail, that you want to be correct in all aspects of your ride, and that you are going to put forth a great test.

After your practice session is completed for the pre-show day, get your horse ready for the show ring.

Clipping

A show horse looks best with a clear bridlepath, trimmed fetlocks, clean throatlatch and muzzle, and trimmed ears. However, your own horsekeeping routine will determine how extreme your clipping will be.

A show horse looks best with a clear bridlepath, trimmed fetlocks, clean throatlatch and muzzle, and trimmed ears.

European dressage riders leave whiskers, eyelashes, and ears unclipped, as their horses spend a great deal of time in pasture and need these feelers to protect them from injury and help them get around. You, however, can vary this so that your horse has adequate pasture protection and fly protection and still looks good. If you stable your horse, or can provide other ways to protect him, you can remove as much hair as you feel comfortable with.

Trim your horse's bridlepath no more than 2½ inches wide, just so the crownpiece of the bridle has room between the forelock and mane. If you choose to clip your horse's ears, only trim the outside and along the edge of the ear, allowing the inside hair to protect him from dust, debris, and flying pests. Be sure to clean the ears well with a slightly damp sponge to get rid of any dirt.

The coronary band and fetlock areas should be trimmed as well. Carefully shave white socks, because white hair is usually more coarse than dark hair and mistakes will show up more easily. Try not to shave too deeply—you'll see the pink skin underneath if you do.

The Tail

While your horse can sport a natural tail, dressage horses often have tails that are banged and "pulled." A banged tail is blunt cut straight across, which often gives the tail a thicker appearance. To bang the horse's tail, carefully pick and brush it out until all tangles have been removed. Have a friend lift the horse's tail up from its resting position and place her arm underneath the tailbone so that you will get more of an accurate picture of how short the tail will be when the horse is in motion, carrying his tail higher than in the resting position. Gather the end of the tail together, and cut straight across, well below the hocks. Ideally, a banged tail will hang at the fetlocks, but any area between the hocks and fetlocks is fine. Your helper can also come to the rescue in case the horse decides to swat at a fly and ruin your cut. Leave the tail natural if the horse's tail is thin or only tapers to about hock level.

Pulling the tail involves a lot of work and patience. Hairs are removed from the sides of the dock either by actually pulling them or by using clippers. If you decide to pull your horse's tail, it will take a couple of years for those hairs to grow long again, so make sure this is the look you want. If you ever want to braid the tail (for instance, for a hunter show) you will not be able to.

A pulled tail is short on the underside, for about 5 inches down, along the sides of the tail. The pulled section ends just where the hairs fall over naturally. It should be thinned at the top, but not completely bare.

You should pull the tail after you have exercised your horse so that his pores are open and it will be less painful. To pull out tail hairs, grasp only a few hairs at a time. While the tail isn't as sensitive as your own scalp, it is more sensitive than the mane, so don't rip out large tufts of hair. Quickly pull outward, not up or down. Switch sides often for balance and to give the pulled area a rest so the horse doesn't get sore. You may shorten the hairs along the side by breaking them off with your pulling comb or an old electric clipper blade, in $1/4$-inch increments.

A painless, more humane alternative to pulling hair manually is trimming the tail using electric clippers. Using a very sharp pair of clipper blades, begin at the top of the dock and clip with the lay of the hair. Do not press down hard because you will shear off too much tail. Taper the area you are trimming so that it naturally blends into the longer tail hairs. Go along the sides of the dock closely, and then gradually let the top hairs blend longer. To maintain a tail that is clipped, you'll only have to spend a few minutes every two weeks to get it into shape. That way the tail won't get bushy.

If you don't want your horse to have a pulled tail, you can still get somewhat the effect of pulling by wrapping the tail before the show. Apply a tail wrap using Vetrap or some other cohesive bandage evenly (but not tightly) to a tail dampened with water and setting gel, and then let it dry. Pull the wrap off before your warm-up, and it will have the thin, contoured look of a pulled tail for the show ring. Do not leave a tail wrap on for longer than a couple of hours, and never wrap it tight enough for it to cut off circulation.

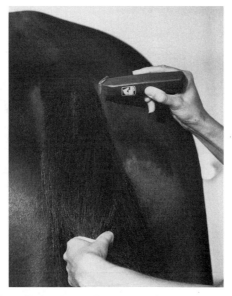

For the look of a pulled tail, use electric clippers as a painless, more humane alternative to pulling hairs manually.

Bathing

It is best to wash your horse in an area with very little breeze so he doesn't catch a chill, particularly if you don't have access to warm water. Gather together your bucket, sponges, shampoo, conditioner, and sweat scraper. For best results, dilute your shampoo in a bucket of warm water.

Wet your horse down by first spraying his legs, then work up to the shoulder, barrel, and haunches. Use your hands or a washing mitt to help work the water in: it makes the shampoo penetrate to the skin if the horse is thoroughly wet.

Using a sponge, mitt, or brush, soap up your horse with the suds from the bucket. Shampoo applied straight out of the bottle can result in your having to rinse for a lot longer, and it can

Use your hands or a washing mitt to help work the water and shampoo in. Pay attention to places where dirt shows up most: the croup, saddle area, legs, and white areas.

be irritating to horses with sensitive skin. A sponge with a scrubbing side will help the suds get in deep.

Pay particular attention to the areas that get most dirty: the croup, the saddle area, the legs, and white areas. A square dressage pad will show dirt around the edges if the horse is not well scrubbed. Your horse's mane should be washed but not conditioned, because a conditioned mane is very difficult to braid. The dirt and scurf present in the mane will be more noticeable after braiding, so scrub down to the scalp. Your horse's tail will not be braided, so condition it as you wish.

Scrub the hooves with a plastic or natural brush. Do not use any abrasive materials, otherwise you will remove the periople, the protective outer layer that keeps moisture out of the hoof. Wash the horse's face with water from a bucket, warm if available, and a soft sponge. Do not use shampoo unless it is a baby shampoo and you are careful to rinse it away *completely.* Horses resent being squirted in the face, and working with a sponge lets you inspect his face for fungus, as well as clean the eyes, ears, and nostrils more thoroughly. It also allows you to manually check for any unclipped areas that you may have missed.

Braiding

If your ride times are later in the day, you can braid the day of the show. Generally, you'll have a morning ride time, so you will need to braid the night before to give yourself time to concentrate on your warm-up in the morning. Tie your horse in an area that is shady and breeze-free. You will need:

- yarn (twenty-five pieces, about 20 inches in length, in a color that matches your horse's mane)

- latch hook

- sponge and bucket or spray bottle

- Braid-Aid

- comb

- fly spray

- setting gel or hair spray

Start with a mane that is a hand's width in length (about 4 inches) and evenly pulled so that it is the same thickness throughout. Dressage horses sport fewer but larger braids than hunters. You will probably only put in eighteen to twenty-five braids on the dressage horse, but they will be thick. Dressage horses are braided on either side of the neck. Start with a section of damp hair a little more than an inch wide. If the freshly washed mane seems a little too slippery, add setting gel or hair spray so the hair will be easier to handle. Divide that section into three hanks (smaller segments), and begin to braid. About

Begin by sectioning off and braiding the mane. Add yarn into each braid about halfway down and then tie off the end.

Place a latch hook or braid puller at the base of the braid and push it through to the underside.

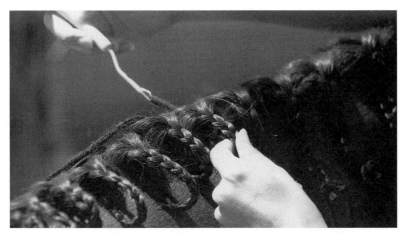

Run the yarn through the open latch, close the latch, and pull straight up so that the yarn comes through the top of the braid.

Then tie off the braids with half a square knot underneath and then a full square knot on top.

Finish the braids by cutting off the excess yarn.

halfway down, add a piece of yarn to the braid from the back. Go as far down the braid as you can, and then end with a slip knot, or wrap the yarn front to back, then tie in a square knot. Continue until the entire mane is braided and tied off with yarn.

Then take your latch hook or braid puller and place it at the very base of the braid, right in the center. Run the yarn through the open latch, close the latch, and pull straight up. The yarn will come through the top of the braid and out. After this step, tie off the braids with half a square knot underneath and then a full square knot on top.

If you have never braided a mane before, it is a good idea to practice with your horse a couple of times a week by putting in three or four braids at a time (take them out afterward). This will help your coordination, and with repetition, you'll actually become more skilled and confident at your task. The only way you'll get better at braids is by doing them.

If the thought of braiding with yarn seems like too much for your braiding talents, you can use elastic bands to secure the braids instead. Choose the small bands available in tack shops that most closely match your horse's mane color. Secure the end of a three-strand plait with one band. Then fold the braid under and tie it up with another band.

Use fly spray to help your horse from becoming agitated. A horse that tosses his head around will make your job more difficult, so make him as comfortable as you can, and reward him for standing still by completing your job as quickly as possible.

If your horse has a super neck and head carriage, you may want to tape the finished yarn- or elastic band–braids with white tape or reusable plastic braid wraps, both available at tack shops. This should be done on show morning. Your braid job must be impeccable, however, and your horse must have a really well-built neck, otherwise any weaknesses will be accentuated.

Braids should not be left in longer than forty-eight hours; if left in longer, the mane hairs will begin to fall out. Take the braids out when your show is over.

By now, your horse has had a fairly long day, so put a sheet on him when you're ready to put him up for the night. Now is the time to get the rest of your equipment ready for the next day.

Leather Care

Once your horse is clean and shiny, you need to make your tack match your horse. There are many different leather-care products, but make sure that you are familiar with whatever you use so it doesn't make tack slippery or sticky. Remember that some one-step products contain lanolin, which can leave a whitish residue. That can be a problem for dressage tack, which is usually black.

If you have a dressage bridle that is padded and lined with white, use a cloth or a soft brush with your leather cleaner to remove any grime and make the white stand out. If you like to get fancy, a separate show browband with a brass or rhinestone inlay can be added for sparkle. Take the leathers and irons off your saddle, and scrub the irons (and the bit) to make sure that dirt and stains are removed. Dip your Fillis pads (the stirrup pads that fit into your irons) in a water and bleach solution for a few minutes, and use an old toothbrush to get into crevices. Then scrub the pads back to their original white.

After your leather cleaner, use a conditioner to nourish the leather. You don't want to add an oil because oil will invariably come off on your white breeches. Also, wipe the reins thoroughly after cleaning to be sure they are not slippery or sticky.

Invest in a saddle cover and bridle bag if you are not going to take a huge tack trunk with you. You can make do by

Gather your grooming supplies, tack, longeing equipment, accessories, and anything else you may need, and check off each item on your list.

draping a large beach towel over your clean saddle and by placing your clean bridle in a pillow case and tying it closed with a shoelace.

If you have access to the trailer your horse will be hauled in and it has a lock on the storage compartment, pack the night before. It is easier to gather your grooming supplies, tack, longeing equipment, accessories, and anything else you may need when you don't have to rush the morning of the show. Fill the haynets or manger. Check off each item on your list, and take into account the weather. If it will be cold, bring a cooler for your horse and rain gear for yourself (regulation rain gear is a transparent or conservative-color raincoat and a hat cover); if it will be hot, don't forget the fly spray.

When you get home, lay out your show clothes for the morning. You can wear your dressage whites to the show grounds, safely covered by sweat pants or the like, or else you can change on the grounds. It is often easier to wear the baggy clothes over your show attire than to try to change in a tiny bathroom stall or porta-john.

You're finished! Now you can relax after your long day of preparation. With all of the work that you have accomplished in the last few days, it should be easy to fall right asleep, but if you are lying awake in eager anticipation of the next day's events, you're not alone. You can bet that there are a bunch of other riders all over the country waiting for sleep to come before their big day, too.

What the Well-Dressed Dressage Horse Wears

The show horse looks conservative and sophisticated. Everything about the picture says elegance. While basic black is most often seen in the show ring, the horse should be tacked up in the color that looks best on him. Chestnut horses often look better in a dark Havana brown than black. The bridle is usually padded and lined with white. This looks good on horses with just a little star or snip on their face (or no markings at all), but can look a little overdone if the horse has a bald face or heavy blaze.

Fancy stitched nosebands are fine for hunters but look out of place on a dressage horse. All the buckles on the near side of the bridle should be close together. The noseband and the browband should not be crooked. The flash should fit into the chin groove. Plain reins or reins with stops are more appropriate than laced reins. All the straps should be fastened, with their leather keepers in place.

The saddle should be placed over a spotless square dressage pad. The show pad can be white or black (whichever looks

(continues)

best against the horse) and can have contrasting piping. Any other colors or emblems on the pad can be added if done tastefully, but it just depends on how conservative you'd like to be.

Girths are generally of the short variety. If you use a girth cover, make sure it is as clean as the saddle pad and doesn't accentuate any conformational flaws. Girths should always have the billets tucked into the keepers, and if these need to be secured, they can be taped down discreetly with black electrical tape. Some short girths have buckle-concealing flaps that make the billets look neater.

Braids are thick and made with the same color yarn as the mane. Braid tape should be used only on excellent braid jobs. Apply braid tape the morning of the show.

The dressage horse's hooves can be left natural, but many riders use hoof polish, either black or clear, for a shiny presentation. Hoof dressings are a compromise, but by the time you do your first lap around the arena, your horse's feet will be covered in dirt anyway. To get the perfect shine without looking patent-leather phony, apply hoof-black lacquer the day before the show, and then add a hoof dressing before beginning your class.

The Search for Hard-To-Find Apparel

Have you been searching for show attire but haven't had much luck finding what you need in your immediate area? If you're like some riders, you may not have access to a good selection, or your size is not readily available.

Several equine catalog companies with good exchange or return policies operate in North America and carry a variety of dressage products, including apparel and tack.

In cases like these, you can ask your tack shop to special order for you. They will contact their distributors for the items you request and get them in for you. This is a good idea if they will let you return items if they don't fit you correctly. But you may want a different alternative.

Several equine catalog companies with good exchange/return policies operate in North America. They carry a wide range of styles and prices not only on apparel but on tack, too. As long as you follow their return policy, these companies present a no-hassle way to purchase through the mail. Most of them have toll-free numbers for ordering, and if you need things in a hurry, they can ship overnight for an additional fee. Look in equine magazines for catalog companies' advertisements.

Show Checklists

Tack and Equipment

☐ Shipping boots/wraps

☐ Poll cap/head bumper

☐ Leather trailering halter/breakaway halter

☐ Chain

☐ Longe line

☐ Longe whip

☐ Polo wraps or protective exercise boots

☐ Cooler/sheet

☐ Saddle soap/sponge

☐ Saddle

☐ Clean pad

☐ Girth

☐ Bridle

☐ Sweat scraper

☐ Grooming kit: brushes, hoof pick, curry comb, sponge, tail brush, towels

☐ Hoof polish

☐ Fly repellent

☐ Show Sheen

☐ Hoof dressing (optional)

Rider

- ☐ Helmet or hunt cap
- ☐ Boots/boot pulls/boot jack
- ☐ Spurs
- ☐ Dressage whip
- ☐ Gloves
- ☐ Coat
- ☐ Socks
- ☐ Shirt
- ☐ Stock tie/stock pin
- ☐ Breeches
- ☐ Hair accessories/net/hair spray
- ☐ Makeup and mirror
- ☐ Tissues
- ☐ Money
- ☐ Cooler with ice and food
- ☐ Paperwork (tests, Coggins results, membership cards, etc.)

Trailering Items

- ☐ Trailer tie
- ☐ Extra lead rope
- ☐ Water bucket

(continues)

☐ Haynet/bag

☐ Hay/feed

☐ Electrolytes

☐ Pitchfork/muck bucket

☐ Liniment

☐ Chairs/umbrella

Miscellaneous

☐ Bedding

☐ Extra bucket

☐ Farm/stable nameplate

☐ First-aid kit

☐ Blanket/pillow

☐ Curtains for stall to act as changing room

Chapter Nine

Success on
Show Day

The day that you've worked for has finally arrived. If you're starting out in the Introductory classes, you will probably be one of the first rides. Training-Level tests, because of their popularity, may be scattered throughout the day or held within the same block of time. First- and Second-Level classes are usually scheduled mid-day to late afternoon. Assuming that you are scheduled for morning rides, you'll have to be up pretty early to arrive in time for your horse to warm up successfully.

Start your day off right by having something nutritious to eat. Just as you wouldn't think of filling your horse's haynet with poor-quality hay, or his feeder with sugar cubes, you shouldn't think that you'll perform well on jitter-building coffee, greasy donuts, or worse—nothing.

It's hard to think of eating anything if you are a little nervous, but you need to keep up your energy, or you'll get fatigued after your first warm-up. A muffin, bagel, or toast with jam can be an easy and quick energy source. Cereals, with the exception of the sugary ones, topped with fruit and lowfat milk are also a good choice. Breakfasts that include bacon and eggs, hash browns and sausage, and the like are loaded with fat, as are sweet rolls, donuts, and pancakes with butter and syrup. Once you have something nourishing in your system, you can address the challenges of the day better.

Determine how much time you will need before your test by adding up the time it will take to accomplish your morning tasks, including:

- Preparing your horse for trailering

- Loading, hauling, and unloading your horse

- Unpacking and checking in at the show office

- Longeing

- Grooming and tacking up

- Warming up for the test

Be generous with your estimates. You want to have a leisurely warm-up instead of a panicked "You're in the ring next!" scenario.

It is good to have a helper, be it your groom, a friend, or your driver, so that you can rely on another individual when packing, loading, and getting ready at the show. Arrange for your assistant to meet you at your stable. Arrive at the barn with everything you need with you. If you didn't have access to the trailer to pack your items the night before, do this before you load your horse. Go over your checklists to make sure you don't leave anything behind.

Get your horse ready to travel by putting on his shipping boots or bandages. If your horse tends to step on longer bandages or boots, wrap his legs down to the pastern and then add bell boots to protect his coronary band. Trailer in a leather halter because it will give way in an emergency, and thread a poll cap through the crownpiece in case your horse has the tendency to bump his head against the top of the trailer. Place a travel sheet on him if it is cool enough.

Load up your horse without rushing him. If you know your horse has difficulty loading, allow for more time early in the day, and never force him angrily. Any trailering difficulties

On show morning, outfit your horse for travel and, without rushing him, load him up.

should be worked out before the show, as show day is not the time to try to reeducate your horse. Tie your horse with a trailer tie that has two "panic snaps" for emergency situations, and let your horse eat the hay in the trailer. If the hay in your area is particularly dusty, dampen it so that when the trailer is in motion, the horse won't be breathing in dust particles. You are now on your way.

Never try to make up time on the road with a horse in tow. Just one bad ride can turn a horse into a problem traveler, so allow extra time for traffic tie-ups. The driver—whether it's your friend or you—should plan all turns and braking well in advance, and make lane changes as smoothly as possible.

After you arrive at the show grounds, unload your horse in a quiet area where the ground is fairly level. It would be great to park in the shade, but if there are no trees, try to park so that your horse can be kept cool in the shade of the trailer. Give your horse a chance to settle down from the ride by walking him around your immediate area. Set up a filled haynet, tie your horse to the trailer, and let him have his breakfast and relax.

While your assistant stays with your horse, pick up your number and ride schedule from the show office. If you have to show any membership cards from the USDF or your state or local dressage chapter, this is the time to do so. Ask any necessary questions at this time, such as:

- Where is the nearest place to fill water buckets?

- Where are the rest rooms?

- Am I parked in an area that is set aside for visitors, or do I need to move?

- Are there wash racks available to show participants?

Check that your ride times match what you were originally told. Occasionally, you may have a different ride time than you expected due to error or changes in schedule.

Return to your horse, and get your equipment ready to go. First, you will want to determine what type of mood your horse is in. If he looks as though he is settling in nicely, you can probably just groom him up when the time comes, and head to the warm-up arena. However, if he's frisky and looks as though he wants to tear the side off the trailer, you may want to longe him. Put protective legwear on him and head out to the longeing area. Most dressage shows will not allow you to longe in the warm-up arena, but will instead provide a separate area, perhaps in a different ring or an open field, to get the bucks out. If your horse just has a little extra energy, you may not need more than a few minutes of longeing in either direction, but if he is upset or misbehaving, you may want to take him well out of the path of others and let him go. Don't let him run around like mad, though, because he may not be used to the feel of the different footing and may injure himself. Keep him under control, and simply let him blow off a little steam.

Next, take him back to the trailer and groom him and tack up. You can keep his leg wraps or boots on during your warm-up, but you must remove them before entering the arena for your test or else you will be disqualified. Also, you can only warm up in equipment that you are allowed to show in. AHSA rules permit the use of running martingales (with a snaffle only) as well as single side reins only while longeing. You cannot use any training devices, such as draw reins, side reins, balancing reins, or "neck stretchers" while you are in the saddle. The ring steward will check for any illegal equipment, including bits, nosebands, training equipment, and leg boots.

The warm-up arena can be chaotic if riders do not follow dressage protocol, so always try to be courteous to the other riders.

During your warm-up, try to be courteous to the other riders, even if they are not doing the same for you. Riders tend to be in their own little world at a show, and most don't mean to be rude, but some people may not understand the do's and don'ts of dressage protocol. If you are prepared, you will feel better for knowing what is correct.

If you ride at an equestrian center, you know that the same rules of traffic that govern our roads also apply to the arena. If you train at home, however, it can be a little disconcerting to be in a sea of riders, all going different directions in controlled chaos. To avoid pile-ups, pass left shoulder to left shoulder, and let those who are doing extensive suppling patterns, lateral work, or advanced movements have the inner part of the arena. In general, pass on the inside of riders going in the same direction as you. Keep your eyes up, and try to prepare for unexpected stops. Your horse may get caught in a bottleneck, but try to maneuver him so that you can concentrate on getting him relaxed and moving forward off of your aids, and keeping him straight and supple. Your horse will no doubt put you to the test, either by being a little nervous or by acting out of sorts in his new surroundings. Don't worry, though, he may surprise you by being calm, responsive, and ready to shine.

Keep an eye out for the ring steward or manager who oversees the running of the show. If the classes are on time, you should be prepared to ride in at the gate at your specified hour. However, if things have fallen behind, you need to know that as well so you don't wear out your horse before your class. If riders ahead of you scratch, you have the choice of moving up and riding sooner, but you don't have to. Your teacher, groom, or friend can help you keep track of where you stand with time.

When a show has a very large turnout, the rides can easily fall behind schedule. Delays can occur if riders go off course, if someone rides out of order, or if show management did not plan enough time between tests for the previous rider to exit the arena and the judge to finish up his or her comments. Have patience in situations like these because they are not usually the norm.

Remember to remove leg wraps or boots from your horse before you go in for your test. Once the rider scheduled before you has halted and saluted at the end of his or her test, you may enter the ring and make your round outside the dressage court. Determine which direction to ride around by the direction of the first turn in your test. For instance, if you ride rising trot and track right at C in your test, you want to track right in your warm-up lap.

Who Are the Judges?

Depending upon the type of show you are attending, whether it is a schooling, open, or rated show, you will see different classifications of judges.

They include:

"S" judge—Senior judge.   This judge is allowed to officiate in all AHSA and FEI-level dressage classes at recognized shows.

"R" judge—Registered judge.   This person may judge alone at any competition in the division in which he is registered. Registered dressage judges may not officiate in classes above Fourth Level.

"r" judge—Recorded judge.   This judge may not officiate at the Third Level and above.

"L" judge—Learner judge.   The L program has been designed by the USDF to help develop new dressage judges, as well as to promote a better understanding of what judges are looking for at Training through Second levels. Learner judges can often be found officiating at schooling shows or working with an R judge at recognized shows.

FEI judges are licensed to officiate at international shows:

"C" judge—Candidate judge.   This judge, who is a candidate for the full FEI license, can judge at international competitions.

"I" judge—International judge.   This person is allowed to judge at most FEI-sanctioned competitions as well as championships.

"O" judge—Official judge.   This title is reserved for an individual who can judge and be president of the ground jury anywhere, including all championships and the Olympics.

Your Test

Your time has come to ride your test in front of the judge. After the judge rings the bell, you have sixty seconds to enter the arena at A. This will give you ample time to ride around the perimeter of the dressage court, so don't feel as though you must whip around in a U-turn just because you passed A when the bell rang. Develop your energy in your warm-up lap, and try to get your horse as prepared as possible before entering at A. If you pass the judge, a simple nod or smile is fine—don't joke around with the scribe or the judge even if it is a schooling show. If the judge is being jovial, you may relax and return the tone, but generally, keep a workmanlike, pleasant attitude and appearance. At this time the scribe will check your number to verify that you are the correct rider for the ride time.

The judge's first impression is important, so try to make your centerline as straight as possible. Look dead ahead, and maintain even leg and rein pressure to prevent your horse from weaving down the middle of the arena. Come to a full halt, then salute with your free hand (grasp the reins and whip in one hand, which is sometimes a little tricky for show-nerved riders). Take a relaxing breath, and then move off into your test.

You may have someone call your test if you feel it will help you be more confident while riding. The judge will not mark you down for having a reader. However, it is good to get into the habit of riding your test without that crutch. The reader is not allowed to say anything except the actual test movements.

During your test, it is important to keep a clear mind. Sometimes, you may draw a blank and be utterly perplexed as to your next movement. This happens to all levels of riders, so don't feel bad if you forget where your transitions should be or if you sail by the designated markers. If you do hear the judge's bell, halt, get instruction on what movement you missed, and continue on. If you can't hear the judge because

During your test, keep a clear mind, and stay focused so you remember the next movement.

you are down by A and she has a thin little voice, it is all right to ride forward to C for directions.

In the event that you do go off course, it is not the end of the world. Try to recoup your professional attitude, and don't let it bother you. You only lose two points off that movement. Also, if your horse completely blows a movement by a spook or shy, don't lose heart. It's only one of many different elements of the test, and you can make up the loss by just forgetting about that one movement and mentally moving on. If you dwell on the bad thing—"I can't believe he broke into a canter instead of a trot"—you may sacrifice your success for the rest of your ride.

If you make an "error of the test," which means that you did something slightly different from what was on the test, such as making your transition a letter early or forgetting to post the trot, the judge will probably not stop the test, but just deduct points from that movement.

Some other things may get you in trouble. If you go off course once in your test, it is only two points off, but the second time you'll get four points deducted, and on the third you'll get eight points off. If you go off course four times, you will be eliminated. You'll also be eliminated if your horse leaves the arena. If you talk or make any sounds to your horse, the judge must deduct two points per violation, which can get pretty costly if you're extra chatty!

If things are going rather badly for you, for example, your horse is rearing up or refuses to move forward to C because the judge's booth is much too scary, you must ask for permission from the judge before you can dismount or leave the arena.

After your final salute, allow your horse to walk forward a few steps toward the judge. Many judges like to tell you their impressions of your ride, or they may want to ask about the breed and age of your horse. Most judges, however, will refrain from speaking to the rider until all riders have finished a particular test.

If you are riding another test close in time to the one you just finished, keep your horse tacked up. If you have a longer break in between tests, your horse's attitude will be better if you untack him for that period. Make sure that he has ample water, particularly if he has worked up a sweat, but let him walk and cool down first before letting him drink. Sponge down his coat to remove the sweat that has accumulated.

Remember to keep yourself hydrated throughout your day as well. The old cliché of "eight glasses of water a day" pertains to your show schedule, too. Drink water in small amounts, and take a sports bottle along so you can drink while in the saddle. Stay away from caffeinated sodas, such as colas. The caffeine acts as a stimulant—something you probably won't need on show day. If you want an extra energy boost, athletic performance drinks are a good source of carbohydrates and sodium replacement.

Your second test gives you a chance to build on what you began in the first test. Your horse will have had exposure to the arena, and you will know what it feels like to ride in the manège in front of the judge. If you felt that there were areas lacking in the first test, try to focus on making them better. Your final salute marks the end of your first show day!

While you are waiting for your second class to close and for your test results, you can take out your horse's braids and begin to pack up your belongings. A seam ripper is good for cutting through yarn, but make sure that you're slicing through wool only and not mane! Pick up all of the yarn ends that you pull out, and put them in the trash. Look for items that you might have left on the wheel wells of the trailer or on the hitch, and pack them. You don't want them flying onto the highway once you get rolling.

Begin to clean up your area. Find out where the muck heap is so you don't leave piles of manure in the trailer parking area. Gather any loose hay, and put it back in the trailer manger, or dispose of it. Show management appreciates competitors who are conscientious about not leaving a mess.

Check the posted boards or computer print-out for test results.

You will be able to see the results of your test when the class closes and all riders have finished. Let the scorer do her job in peace, and don't ask her for your own scores early. Turn in your show number when you pick up your test. The competitors who received the highest scores in the class will receive a ribbon with their test. The judge's comments on your test sheet are very important because they provide you with valuable insight on what you did during the ride. Most judges are very fair—some are a little lenient, others, a little strict—but all will provide you with helpful criticism of your ride.

The judge's comments on your test sheet are very important because they provide you with valuable insight on what you did during the ride.

Showing gets easier the more often you do it. Just as a green horse becomes seasoned the more times he's out in the ring, so will a green rider. You'll feel great when you return home knowing that what you've been working on all these months has been put to the test, not to mention bringing home good feedback and possibly a ribbon.

In scoring, if you did practically nothing of the movement, for example, your horse bolted down the long side at a dead gallop instead of a working trot, then you would get a 0. Keep in mind that typical scores are in the 5s and 6s. To receive a

Showing becomes easier the more often you compete.

How the Judges Score

10 = Excellent
9 = Very good
8 = Good
7 = Fairly good
6 = Satisfactory
5 = Sufficient
4 = Insufficient
3 = Fairly bad
2 = Bad
1 = Very bad
0 = Not executed

7 or 8 means that you have really done well. Even higher, and the movement must have been spectacular. Don't fret if you see some low marks on your test. Just try to take in the comments that the judge has provided and learn from them.

You also get collective marks after your test that the judge will add on. These are for your horse's gaits—the freedom and regularity of his stride; his impulsion—his forward energy, the elasticity of his stride and his relaxed back; his submission—his willingness while performing the test; and your seat—your position and how effective it was during the test.

The scribe takes down the scores and comments of the judge, then the scorer adds them up and divides that number by the total number of possible points to get the percentage. The higher the percentage, the better the score. You also get collective marks, which have a coefficient of 2, and they are added to your final score.

Why Dressage Tests Change Every Four Years

America is still a relative newcomer to the sport of dressage. As a nation it is still developing ways that help reflect the goals and objectives of the sport in competition. This is why the AHSA dressage tests change every four years.

The changes made by both AHSA and USDF committees are not arbitrary. They are the result of evaluating the previous years' tests and determining what areas should be strengthened and which test movements no longer reflect the objectives of the tests. The committees receive feedback from judges, riders, trainers, and instructors on the effectiveness of past tests and use this information to help develop the new ideals that will carry the dressage community forward into another four-year term.

Dealing with Show Nerves

Even when things are going just fine, you have practiced your test dozens of times perfectly, and you are warming up right on schedule, you may get an attack of show nerves. While it's perfectly normal to suffer from show-day jitters, it's better to find ways to deal with them than give in to them. Some people get so nervous when they are about to go into a test that they equate riding in front of others with public speaking.

When riders are nervous, it affects their ability to ride. Tension is transmitted to the horse within moments of mounting. In contrast, relaxed riders have a calming effect on their horses and usually get a more confident ride out of their mounts.

Much has been said about the power of positive thought. Your subconscious mind helps determine how you will do in the reality of the show ring. Keep positive thoughts and mentally rehearse your tests flawlessly. Picture your horse going around the arena perfectly, with accurate transitions and in a round outline. These techniques will work as a rehearsal for the real event. Also, verbalize your success out loud, and keep any negative phrasing out of your vocabulary. For instance, "He better not kick out at the canter transition" is better changed to "He will have a lovely, smooth canter transition" in your mind. Even when you talk to others about your riding, don't downplay your efforts. It's good to be humble, but you also need to reinforce out loud the fact that you are working toward goals and that you are making wonderful progress.

Distractions such as your kids or dogs are better left at home. Friends and family are also good supporters, but don't feel as though you have to entertain them. You are riding for yourself, and they should realize that you are going to be preoccupied with the task at hand. Occasionally, setbacks will occur, such as when you forget to bring your spurs or your grooming friend arrives too late to help. Try not to let such events ruin your day.

Finally, learn to center yourself and relax before entering the arena. Practice breathing exercises to help yourself calm down. Most people breathe rapidly and shallowly when nervous, which has an adverse physical effect on riding. Breathing from the diaphragm is very helpful, however.

Singers learn to breathe from the diaphragm, so it is possible to "relearn" breathing. As you inhale, expand your stomach instead of your chest. Concentrate as you exhale, because this is an exercise that helps you to release tension and relax. Deep breathing also helps deepen your seat and relax your back. If you are interested in finding out more about mental training, there are books on psycho cybernetics that can aid your riding.

Elimination from the Competition

A rider can be eliminated from competition for the following reasons:

- Lameness of the horse

- When all four feet of the horse leave the arena

- When a horse has his tongue tied down

- When a horse-and-rider combination does not enter the arena within sixty seconds after the bell has rung

- When a horse resists for longer than twenty seconds, which prohibits the test from proceeding

- When a rider displays cruelty to the horse

- When illegal equipment is used

If You Need to Scratch

Annoying things happen: your horse may lose a shoe, you may come down with an allergic reaction, or your horse may step on a stone. If you need to scratch from one or both of your classes, inform show management as soon as possible. According to AHSA rules, scratches must be processed by their official rules. You must obtain permission from the show management before withdrawing your horse from the competition or leaving the show grounds before all of your classes are over.

Treat the Show Officials with Respect

Your test may provide you with more questions than answers, so if you want further explanation about your test sheet, you can meet with the judge after arrangements have been made through the show's technical delegate or show committee. If there is a problem at the show, you should inform management, but do not go on the attack. If you have had a good day, let show management know that, too, particularly with smaller schooling shows where most of the help is unpaid volunteers.

Going to Multi-Day Shows

Once you get the hang of showing, try your hand at events that are farther away from your home base. This may include shows that require you to stable your horse on the show grounds overnight. By being practical and planning ahead, you can attend overnight shows and not break your budget.

The prize list will let you know the cost of overnight stabling. Find out what type of stabling is available, and call show management if you have any questions. You may be able to put your horse in a posh, airy box stall, or you might end up in portable stables. Your horse might be placed in a pipe stall as well.

With your regular checklists, include the following items, and label them to avoid losing them:

☐ Flashlight/fluorescent lantern

☐ Garden hose

☐ Extra buckets

☐ Tack hooks/chairs

☐ Extra feed in sealed containers/bale covers

☐ Stall nameplate with emergency numbers

☐ Stall bedding

☐ Locking tack trunk

☐ Extra lead ropes or cross-ties

When you arrive on the show grounds, it may be nighttime. Many temporary stabling locations at shows are not well lit, so your lantern will come in handy when you are unloading. First, investigate where your horse's stall will be, and then check it out thoroughly. Inspect it for any rough edges, nails, or protruding boards. Look over the floor if it is bare, and make sure there are no dangerous holes that must be filled in before you spread your horse's bedding.

USDF Regions

Region One   Delaware, Maryland, New Jersey, North Carolina, Pennsylvania, Virginia, Washington, D.C.

Region Two   Illinois, Indiana, Kentucky, Michigan, Ohio, West Virginia, Wisconsin

Region Three   Alabama, Florida, Georgia, South Carolina, Tennessee

Region Four   Iowa, Kansas, Minnesota, Missouri, Nebraska, North Dakota, South Dakota

Region Five   Arizona, Colorado, Eastern Montana, New Mexico, Utah, West Texas, Wyoming

Region Six   Alaska, Idaho, Western Montana, Oregon, Washington

Region Seven   California, Hawaii, Nevada

Region Eight   Connecticut, Maine, Massachusetts, New Hampshire, New York, Rhode Island, Vermont

Region Nine   Arkansas, Louisiana, Mississippi, Oklahoma, Texas

Don't overdo it with shavings or straw for an overnight show. Simply make sure that the floor has a bit of cushion, and a deep enough layer to make your horse feel comfortable, but you don't have to bank up the sides.

Unload your horse in a quiet area, and let him walk around for a bit, then turn him into his stall. He will be tired from his journey and may be a little unsettled in new surroundings. He will need time to get accustomed to the new sights and sounds of the show grounds. Find out where the water is, and fill him a bucket if there is no automatic waterer in his stall. Check in with the show secretary, and pick up your number, and also check for any new or important postings regarding competitors.

Get your horse's feed for the evening together, and see if he'll eat. Spend time with him, and then look around the show grounds. Most shows will have a designated area for the muck heap and for horse washing, so find out where these areas are. Find out if guests are allowed to turn out their horses and where the turnout rings are located. Some facilities are off-limits to show participants, so don't raise the ire of the permanent boarders by availing yourself of their wash racks, hot-walkers, or turnout rings unless you are allowed to use them.

Many other participants will be arriving at the same time that you do, so make friends with your neighbors. You'll find that most show competitors are friendly, and if they are not outright sociable, they will at least be civil.

Secure all of your belongings, and don't let valuables such as your purse sit out on top of your tack trunk or on the seat of your car. Keep your tack trunk locked, and if you are sharing a "tack room" area (which is often another stall), you might consider investing in tags or nameplates for your tack to identify it easily.

Keep your area clean and organized. You will be sharing the aisles with many other folks, so set a good example, and don't let your area get sloppy or out of control. When you pack up and head for home, double-check your list to make sure that you have everything you brought. Items such as pitch-forks, water buckets, lead ropes, and tack hooks are easily left behind if you don't make a conscious effort to bring them home.

Showing away from your home base, and the camaraderie that you'll experience, will make for many lasting memories!

"Qualifying" Your Horse

The USDF has implemented other ways to earn rewards. Riders of all levels can receive cumulative awards. At the highest level, the USDF Gold Medal, a rider must achieve four scores of 60 percent or better, two at Intermediate I and/or Intermediate II, and two at Grand Prix, each from two different judges for two different rides. The USDF Silver Medal requires four scores of 60 percent or better, two at Fourth Level and two at Prix St. Georges, each from two different judges for two different rides. The Bronze Medal requires six scores of 60 percent or better, two at First Level, two at Second Level, and two at Third Level, each from two different judges for two different rides. The Qualified Rider Award requires four scores of 60 percent or better at Training Level, earned at a minimum of two different competitions, from four different judges for four different rides.

You can qualify your horse for regional championships as well by earning two qualifying scores in an official qualifying class at two separate AHSA/USDF-recognized competitions from two different judges. The percentages vary, depending upon what level you ride, so contact your state dressage organization or the region to find out if your horse is eligible for the championships.

New Opportunities at Shows

DRESSAGE SEAT EQUITATION   This is a class in which you are judged on your position and how it influences the horse. The goal in this class is for the rider to develop a beautiful as well as effective seat. It is currently modeled after the Medal division in hunter-seat equitation classes. There is classical equitation, but instead of having a certain "style" that becomes fashion, the DSE class has functional reasons for the position. This is a relatively new class and is not available at all shows. However, the dressage regions are working to include an equitation class at the Regional Championships.

Dressage Seat Equitation classes are open to riders competing up to Second Level. Riders show their horses at the walk, trot, and canter in both directions of the arena. While all the riders will be judged at the same time, the judge may ask for a particular rider to perform certain tests. Correct transitions are emphasized.

QUADRILLE   This activity involves groups of four riders (four, eight, sixteen, and so on) and includes a set of movements that are judged both on a compulsory level and as freestyles. Quadrille is growing as dressage looks to interest more spectators in the sport. It encourages riders of all types to participate, and many riders enjoy being part of a team, because there is less pressure when you are not the only rider in the arena. Quadrille has its history in the cavalry, and the public is most familiar with the British Horse Guards, the Canadian Mounted Police, and the Spanish Riding School of Vienna, all of which still practice military movements.

Music is optional in quadrille tests. If you have a favorite marching piece, you can choreograph your team's ride to it.

(continues)

The team's horses may wear boots or bandages, but if one horse wears them, then all must wear the same. The riders should dress in matching outfits. Riding coats, whips, and spurs are optional. In freestyle quadrilles, however, music is mandatory, and emphasis is placed on finding a cohesive musical theme with smooth editing. The program is judged on technical precision, creativity, and artistic presentation. Shows may even offer quadrille classes that allow riders to compete in costume divisions.

PAS DE DEUX   If you have ever wanted to compete with a friend, or even just design a program for two riders, the Pas de Deux is for you. It doesn't matter what level you ride, as these classes are judged on horses within the same level. This way you don't have to worry that your program will be competing against one with Michelle Gibson and Guenter Seidel!

This artistic exercise lets two riders present their horses in a ride set to music. The ride is judged on technical execution and artistic impression. For the technical aspect, the judge evaluates the team as a unit for accuracy of execution and the horses' impulsion and submission. The artistic scoring is based on how well the Pas de Deux is choreographed, its musicality, and how well the two horses and riders work together.

The Pas de Deux is a five-minute program in which the two riders must enter the ring as a pair and end their program as a pair. The riders can perform any figures, patterns, combinations, or transitions related to the level they are showing, but if they include movements "above the level," they will have points deducted. Certain movements are forbidden at particular levels because they reflect higher-level work.

As you see, dressage offers many options and challenges.

Chapter Ten

Moving Forward, Moving Up

*A*s you have learned, a dressage horse is not made overnight. Months of diligent training, a sensible schedule, and consistent care go into each dressage athlete. You can aid your horse's progress by giving him the extra attention that a performance horse needs.

As you increase your demands on your horse, counter them by providing him with the energy resources that he'll need to draw from. Correct nutrition improves a horse's feeling of well being, as well as the way his body and mind function.

A horse that is fit nutritionally will be able to cope better with the stress of showing, traveling, and attending clinics. Furthermore, he will be able to recover better after an accident or illness. A horse that is run-down nutritionally will not be able to fight off illness and is more susceptible to breakdowns.

Although your horse won't need the diet of a racehorse, he will still need the right energy-boosting foods. Unlike racehorses or show jumpers, which need quick and fast energy from their food, dressage horses need energy that is released more slowly. Your horse gets his energy from his hay and roughage, along with the right kind of additional feed.

Months of diligent training, a sensible schedule, and consistent care go into each dressage athlete.

Dressage is a hard, gymnastic sport for your horse, and if he is carrying a surplus of fat, it will stress his body unnecessarily. If your horse is not a towering warmblood, do not overfeed him in an effort to emulate the bulk of some of these horses, because you are inviting lameness problems, including laminitis, from the additional weight.

Know What to Feed

When increasing your horse's workload, the first thing you need to address is his diet. Horses that perform mostly light work can get by on a diet of quality hay only. Hard-working horses need to consume more energy so that they have more to expend. If the pasture in your area is below par or nonexistent, and the hay that you feed is of varying quality, supplement your horse's diet with a processed feed to give him the extra energy he needs to perform.

Forage Feeds

A horse needs at least half of his diet to be hay, for roughage to keep him healthy. Hay, also called forage, is vital to your horse's nutritional upkeep. Hay and grass contain cellulose, a form of starch, or carbohydrate, that creates bulk. Fiber, which adds bulk to a horse's diet, is very important because it helps maintain the horse's natural process of digesting food constantly.

Horses kept out on good pasture get much of their roughage from grass. Horses that are stabled or kept in grassless paddocks must depend upon hay or cubes in order to get the roughage necessary to keep their digestion working properly. There are plenty of ways for your horse to get his roughage, whether he is in a pasture or stabled.

Long-stem hay, available with varying consistency depending upon your region and the time of the year, is the most commonly known forage feed. "Certified" hay bales, sold boxed and compressed to half their original size, are certified to be free from weeds. Because of their smaller size and their packaging, they are made with convenience and consistency in mind.

Hay cubes are not just chopped and compressed dry hay. Several hay blends have specialty formulas just for performance horses. Again, consistency and convenience in the product make hay cubes a good alternative to regular baled hay.

Sweet Feeds

Sweet feeds are made from a variety of grains and other ingredients that are bound together with a syrup, often molasses. Most horses will eat a sweetened grain product readily, and won't tire of it as they may do with other processed feeds. When the grains, such as corn, oats, or barley, are crimped or cracked, it helps the horse's digestive system utilize its nutrients.

Not all sweet feeds are alike, so choose them carefully by understanding the ingredients. A sweet feed can be a forage product, a complete feed, or a concentrate. Some sweet feeds have a very high protein content, from 10 to 18 percent. These are usually designed for young, growing horses. Evaluate the minimum percentage of the protein and the maximum percentage of fiber and fat contained in the feed to determine what to add into your horse's nutritional program.

Complete Feeds

Complete feeds are purported by the manufacturers to eliminate the need to feed hay to horses. This can be a welcome relief to horse owners who do not have access to quality hay year-round.

Complete pellets do provide a nutritionally balanced diet as far as carbohydrates, protein, energy, vitamins, and minerals are concerned, but the practical aspect of providing fiber in this form is not desirable. Horses still need roughage, and many intestinal upsets can take place, including colic, if they do not get their forage food. Also, many horses can become unhappy with the lack of bulky roughage to munch on, and as a result develop vices, including cribbing. It is best to feed your horse some hay, even a lower-protein hay such as timothy or oat hay, so that the horse still has access to roughage and has something to chew on to keep him busy and content.

Extruded feeds are those that are processed by cooking the grain at high pressure. This procedure breaks up starch molecules and makes the resulting feed easier to digest. Extruded feeds often look like dry dog food. Horses tend to eat extruded feeds more slowly because of the large, puffy shape of the feed, so incidents of choke or gastric problems are reduced.

Owners who wish to add extra energy to their horse's diet can top dress (add to) their horse's ration with corn or vegetable oil. Fats and oils have more than twice the amount of energy of carbohydrates or protein, so they can be given to a horse for a better hair coat and to increase energy.

Some horse nutritionists claim that because pelleted feeds are super processed, with their ingredients ground up, formed, and dried, they pass through the horse's digestive tract faster than roughage does and therefore leave the horse feeling hungry again sooner. Also, some claim that highly processed feeds may cause intestinal upsets, resulting in colic and laminitis. For these reasons, nutritionists recommend that horses on complete feed diets still be given long-stem hay as part of a complete nutritional program.

Know How and When to Feed

You can tell if your working dressage horse is in proper condition by observing and feeling his body. You should be able to feel his ribs fairly easily, but not actually see them. His neck should be firm but not cresty. There should be no channel running down his spine, and you should be able to feel his pelvis. The hip bones should not jut out, nor should there be hollows at the flanks. If he begins to drop weight, he'll lose it along his rump (getting flatter on each side), and you will actually see his ribs. Any definition in his neck will soon be lost.

Feed your horse by the weight of the food, not by the volume. A scoop of oats and a scoop of corn weigh out differently. By weighing out the food, you can ensure that your horse is getting exactly the amount he needs.

Bran

Bran mashes are a staple of some horse owners' feeding programs, particularly in the winter. It is believed that bran mashes are easy for the horse to digest and are a good reward for hard work or a nice treat on a cold winter day. However, in reality, bran is not that good for your horse. Bran is high in phosphorus and fiber, and low in digestible protein and calcium. It is not easily digested, and it irritates the intestine, which accounts for its famous laxative effect. Every time you give your horse a bran mash, it kills off a portion of the intestinal flora and upsets the delicate balance that keeps his gut working properly.

Supplement Smart

A supplement forms part of the nutritional content of the feed and helps to balance it according to a particular animal's needs. This depends on his condition and health as well as on the diet he's receiving and his work. Your horse may or may not need his diet supplemented by a commercial vitamin or mineral mix. Horses that are most likely to need a supplement are those with poor grazing areas (or none); hard-working performance horses; broodmares in the last three months of pregnancy or the first three months of lactation; rundown or sick animals; and older animals that are finding it harder to metabolize and digest food as they age.

An additive is different from a supplement. An additive is something that is added to your horse's already-balanced diet. Worming medication and chondroitin sulfates, for example, are non-nutritional additives.

Just because your horse is hard-working doesn't mean you need to give him a vitamin supplement. If you end up feeding your horse certain vitamins and minerals, they can actually have an adverse effect on him—or no effect—if they are not properly administered. If you do give your horse a supplement, it is better to use one that provides him with many vitamins, as opposed to one that is vitamin- or mineral-specific. Where supplements are concerned, more is not necessarily good. Follow the dosage instructions on the package, and don't combine multi-vitamin supplements with others unless you have checked with your veterinarian.

Probiotics help with the horse's intestinal flora. These products, which are actually made up of the horse's "good" bacteria that live in the intestine, may be considered as aids to digestion. Probiotics should be regarded as additives rather than as supplements. If your horse experiences problems digesting his food, your veterinarian may recommend probiotics to help rebalance his gut. Probiotics are even recommended by veterinarians to help some horses gain or maintain their optimum weight. They should not be used continuously, however. They are good to give to a horse that has been on antibiotics for a while (antibiotics kill off both the bad and the good bacteria) and animals with a heavy worm burden.

Electrolytes are used to counteract dehydration caused by sweating for prolonged periods. These supplements contain a blend of sodium, chloride, potassium, and magnesium to help replenish the essential nutrients a horse may lose in hot, humid conditions, or under stressful training or showing. They can be fed daily, or can be used when conditions warrant.

The Best Feeding Routine

Horses are designed to process food continually during the day. In the wild, equines forage for about sixteen hours each day and sleep for about five hours. Horses do best when given a little ration of food many times during the day instead of a couple of large meals. Feed your horse often and in small portions. This routine not only helps to keep his good intestinal flora and bacteria thriving, but also prevents him from getting bored and developing behavioral problems.

Any changes in your horse's diet should be made slowly and gradually. Be patient when you are waiting to see any results from a change in your feeding program. Results will not happen overnight, so don't lose heart if you don't see the difference in your horse right away.

Always make sure that your horse drinks an adequate amount of water. Depending on his work and the weather, a horse can drink up to twelve gallons per day and even more in the heat or during hard work. However, much depends on the water content of his feed. As an example, grass will normally be about 75 percent water; although, water content will vary according to weather conditions and the time of year. Fresh grass in a wet spring will be high in water; whereas, shriveled grass in a dry summer or old winter grass will contain much less moisture. Hay and grain mixes such as sweet feed may contain up to only 15 percent water.

Your horse should have fresh water all the time. You may find that your horse likes to wet down his hay in his water bucket before he eats it. This is not unusual, and many horses actually like it when their feed has a higher water content.

Caring for Your Horse

Many things besides a good feeding program will ensure that your horse has a long dressage career. An athletic horse has more opportunity to injure himself or to break down if he is genetically predisposed to certain conditions, so keeping him comfortable and able to perform his work should be your primary concern. Therapeutic programs can help; choose from among those in which you can find a quality professional to administer the treatment.

Chiropractic Care

Chiropractic care for horses is a holistic approach to treating many health and performance issues. Chiropractic is not intended to replace traditional veterinary treatment but rather to complement it. In fact, many chiropractors are DVMs. This and other alternative therapies are quickly gaining popularity in the horse community. Chiropractic focuses mainly on

Most horses that are basically sound will respond quickly to their chiropractic adjustments in one to four sessions.

keeping the spinal column functioning in a healthy manner for the horse.

The horse's spinal column, which is comprised of bones, ligaments, muscles, and nerves, has nearly two hundred joints. The vertebrae are connected by ligaments into a joined column. The spinal cord passes through each vertebra. A complex network of nerves branches off the spinal cord and exits between each pair of vertebrae. The nerves send messages to all the muscles and organs of the body. Numerous muscles are attached to the vertebrae, enabling parts of the spinal column to flex and bend somewhat.

When a certain vertebra is misaligned, "stuck," or moving improperly, it is called a subluxation. A horse with this condition lacks flexibility in his spine and becomes resistant, stiff, and unable to perform his work properly.

A subluxation can occur for many reasons, but usually it is directly related to the back, for example, an ill-fitting saddle that causes the horse pain. However, a subluxation can also be caused by a rider who is not in balance, which causes the horse to hollow his back and not engage properly. Even improperly floated teeth can cause back pain if the horse carries his head in such a way that he inverts his neck and travels hollowly until the subluxation occurs.

A misaligned spine manifests itself in different ways— some obvious, others more subtle. The most obvious sign is that a horse in pain will not travel correctly. He may not be able to engage his hindquarters, and he may hollow his back and extend his head and neck. He might show discomfort or irritation when being saddled or while being ridden. He might wring his tail or pin his ears. He may begin to act up the moment you ask him to do lateral movements or collected work. He might refuse to flex at the poll or come underneath himself.

Subtle signs of a misaligned spine include a change in the horse's behavior or working slightly below his ability. He may show some lameness or be a little off. All of a sudden you may notice that it is hard to stay centered in your saddle. This could be caused by the horse shifting his gaits without a true lameness. You may notice that your horse's shoes are wearing differently or that he may be dragging his toes.

To correct a subluxation, a chiropractor performs a short, rapid thrust onto a vertebra in the direction and angle that will put it into a normal position, realigning the spine. While the horse is a large animal, it doesn't require a great deal of force from the chiropractor to adjust the spine. When the correct angle is found, the adjustment is relatively easy and low-force. Veterinary chiropractors may also manipulate the joints of the legs, the pelvis, the neck, and even the horse's jaw.

Many people believe that it takes several adjustments before the horse's body accepts and maintains the correct alignment, but this is not necessarily true. Indeed, treatment of chronic problems takes a lot longer, but most horses that are basically sound will respond quickly to adjustments in one to four sessions. Many horses experience dramatic change after only one treatment, while others might need continuous therapy. Often the chiropractor will follow up with massage therapy or acupuncture. He may also give the owner some stretching exercises to help keep the aligned horse supple and flexible. By employing these exercises, owners will become more familiar with how their horse's body works.

Because of the demanding work that they have to do, dressage horses benefit from regular maintenance visits from an equine chiropractor. To find a certified equine chiropractor in your area, contact the American Veterinary Chiropractic Association (P.O. Box 249, Port Byron, Illinois 61275-0249; telephone 309-523-3995).

Massage Therapy

Massage not only helps relieve pain, but it can also be part of your horse's overall maintenance program to ensure his continuing health. Like chiropractic, sports massage therapy is not intended to replace traditional veterinary care and should be used only with your veterinarian's approval. Massage therapy cannot cure orthopedic problems, nor can it do away with serious conditions such as laminitis or arthritis. But it can relieve soft-tissue distress, as well as make the horse more comfortable so he can perform without pain.

Massage works on the principle of increasing the blood supply to muscles. In doing so, it delivers needed oxygen to tissues to help eliminate waste products such as lactic acid from them. Massage helps circulation and increases the horse's range of motion. The body's natural pain relievers, endorphins, also are released, causing the horse to feel better.

A horse that needs massage therapy will demonstrate it in one or more ways. He may develop a sudden subtle lameness or become slightly off. He may have been overexerted repeatedly and is simply sore to the touch. He may have muscle spasms, which will eventually cause the muscles to stiffen up. Overused tendons can become seriously inflamed and even develop microtears. A horse that is cooled down too quickly after hard workouts can also become chronically sore.

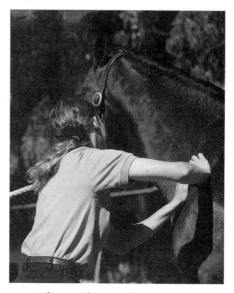

Massage therapy can relieve soft-tissue distress, as well as make the horse more comfortable so he can perform without pain.

Equine massage therapists ask for background information about the horses they work on. They want to know about a horse's previous injuries and current work load. Therapists palpate the horse's soft tissue in order to identify tension below the skin's surface. They also look for irregularities on the horse, for instance, to see if one side is different from the other due to muscle atrophy or injury. The therapist works on sore and spasmodic muscles by using direct pressure techniques along with open-palm compressions or pushing and pulling with a cupped hand. The more complex muscle groups are worked by separating the fibers with cross friction and circular motion.

Therapists often recommend stretching exercises to help the horse's muscles become more flexible, stronger, and less likely to tighten up again.

Laser Therapy

People often think that laser treatments are very invasive or that the laser is used only as a sophisticated surgical instrument. In fact, laser therapy has its place in healing injured tissues—as long as the laser is in the hands of a skilled operator.

Laser equipment uses a special low-intensity beam of light that goes about three millimeters below the surface of the skin. As the light enters the tissues, it stimulates the horse's metabolism, which causes the horse to produce more collagen, the main ingredient of tissue and bone, and speeds healing. Laser therapy is best used for injuries that include wounds, bowed tendons, splints, and torn ligaments. The laser cannot heal serious, deeper injuries, however.

Laser therapy is designed for specific applications and not for overall treatment. At the right setting, laser light causes the horse's body cells to accelerate the healing process, which is why it works so well on open wounds. Laser therapy causes a rapid growth of new cells, so wounds heal much faster than on their own. For soft-tissue injuries, regular treatments such as ice, hydrotherapy, and compression-bandaging are required before treatment with the laser.

Laser therapy increases blood flow and reduces the amount of fluids that build up around an injury. By helping to draw fluids away from the injured area, the laser reduces swelling. The laser is also known to reduce inflammation in injuries located below the skin's surface, thus relieving pain and promoting healing without scar-tissue buildup.

The laser's light usually has two heads, one wide and one narrow, which are moved over the injured area at a very slow speed so they can penetrate the wound or injury. They are different from surgical lasers because their beam is not powerful enough to cut the skin. Laser therapy should only be used on the advice of a veterinarian.

Some veterinarians and chiropractors use the laser light as an alternative to acupuncture needles. In this case, the laser is used to treat a specific condition by way of the acupuncture points rather than by being moved directly over the wounded or injured area.

Acupuncture

The ancient art of acupuncture is resurfacing as a valuable, drug-free healing tool for competitive horses. Special needles are inserted at specific points on the horse's body that are surrounded by nerve endings. When the acupuncturist inserts the needle, he twirls it to start an electrical impulse, or reaction, on the nerve ending. This impulse gets transmitted to the spinal cord and travels to the brain.

The brain then releases different body chemicals, such as endorphins, which increase the tolerance for pain. Basically, these body chemicals help shut off the pain. Acupuncture also promotes self-healing within the horse's body and restores a healthy balance to the horse's system.

This technique should only be performed by a qualified acupuncturist who works specifically with equines.

Dealing with Injuries

Dressage horses are susceptible to injury, particularly soft-tissue injures of the tendons and ligaments. Some injuries are slow to appear, while others can develop suddenly. When your horse does become injured, you need to address the problem immediately and give him the right treatment so he can recover fully. Even if the injury does not appear to be serious, only a veterinarian can make that determination. You must work with your veterinarian to reduce the possibility of damaging, and permanently weakening, your horse because you resume his training too soon.

Many injuries occur because of stress during a workout. Horses that are worked hard before they have warmed up sufficiently are targets for injury, as are those that are pushed beyond their current training level. Horses that do not have enough endurance and become fatigued are also prone to "give out," and this usually results in an injury.

When the superficial and deep flexor tendons or the suspensory ligaments, which are at the back of the cannon bones, are stressed beyond what the horse can handle physically, the fibers of the tendons or ligaments begin to tear or separate. Overextension in a gait, gradual strain over time, or concussion in a deep sand arena can contribute to a bowed tendon or another soft-tissue injury.

It is likely that the horse will exhibit swelling in the injured area. You can feel heat around the injury, and the horse may show signs of being in pain. If you think your horse has suffered a bowed tendon, feel the tendon, and see if you can locate the largest area of swelling. Then pick up your horse's leg and, while supporting the ankle, feel the tendon again to help pinpoint the injury better.

If you notice any of these symptoms, do not continue to work your horse, or you will do further damage. Call your veterinarian immediately, and describe what you have found. The veterinarian will probably want to come and examine your horse. He may instruct you to cool off the injured site with cold water and apply a support bandage or a poultice.

During his examination, the veterinarian may want to use ultrasound on the area of swelling to see how serious the injury is. Your veterinarian will probably recommend anti-inflammatories, including phenylbutazone and dexamethasone, to help reduce the swelling and pain. Usually, the vet will also prescribe stall rest or hand walking. Some exercise regimens that involve trotting have been successful in rebuilding a stronger tendon.

If your horse is coming back from a soft-tissue injury, it is crucial that you do not try to bring him back too early. If he is exercised before the injured area has fully healed, the chances of reinjury are high, and he could permanently damage himself. The horse may appear fine to you, but the torn fibers of the tendons and ligaments need to be fully replaced with healthy, elastic fibers. Have your veterinarian determine when your horse can begin the final road to recovery.

Other Ouchiness

To some degree all horses experience not only injury, but also life-altering changes in their bodies. As horses get older, they are prone to more lameness problems. Arthritis can inflame joints and cause the horse pain. Ringbone, bone spavins, cartilage loss, and bone spurs can reduce the horse's range of motion, and he may be reluctant to work, hard to warm up, or not able to use his body correctly. When these things happen to your equine athlete, you want to do more for him than just mask the pain with a couple of grams of bute. For one thing, long-term use of bute causes irritation to the horse's stomach and intestines. For another, it is not a substance that you can use when you are competing.

Recent success with neutraceuticals, a new classification of nondrug supplements, is prompting more horse owners to use them to help keep their horses going. More scientific research needs to be done in order to support the effectiveness of these products, but you'll find plenty of horse people who swear by them. Neutraceuticals include:

GAGS (GLYCOSAMINOGLYCANS) Synovial fluid helps keep the horse's joints healthy and lubricated. When there is injury or damage within the joint, administering GAGs orally (in powder form mixed in the horse's feed) is reported to help repair damaged cartilage. PSGAGs (polysulfated glycosaminoglycans) are designed to stimulate the production of synovial fluid. Usually products with "flex" in the name contain chondroitin sulfates and are intended to reduce destructive enzymes and contribute to cartilage repair.

ANTIOXIDANTS (VITAMIN E, MSM/METHYLSULFONYLMETHANE) These are reported to help cartilage stay healthy, keeping the joints moving freely. "Free radicals" found within the horse's system as a byproduct of the horse's normal metabolism are thought to be harmful to the horse's tissue. Free radicals are byproducts of regular metabolism as well as byproducts of injury or the repair process. Free radicals are thought to contribute to cancer, possibly. Antioxidants go to the source of the horse's soreness to help heal the injury and kill off the free radicals.

Moving Up

Even though a dressage horse cannot be made overnight, you will see progress as your horse begins to meet your goals, if not quickly, then gradually. Your own riding will also improve greatly. If you have been training and showing at Training Level and doing well at schooling shows, you should immediately try your hand at the larger rated shows.

Don't get scared of your progress. You have opened the door to moving up. It's time to begin working on the next level when your horse is well "confirmed" at his current level. This means that he's accomplished the goals and objectives of his current level.

You've got Training Level's objectives down when:

- Your horse is truly on the bit

- He travels in a round outline, exhibiting a measure of "throughness"

- He moves freely forward on his own, in a steady rhythm

- His muscles are supple and loose

- He exhibits impulsion

- He stretches down to accept the bit's contact

- He does not resist the rider's hands

- He bends in his circles

Your show scores will also reflect that your horse has attained the goals of the level. If you receive scores in the 65th percentile or better, you should try to move your horse up to the next level, which is First.

Moving Up with Music

Do you want to try something new in dressage? Are you looking to develop something unique to express the teamwork you and your horse share? The hottest ticket in dressage may be the musical freestyle, or *kur,* as it is called in German. For the first time in history, the kur was added as an Olympic event at the 1996 Games in Atlanta, Georgia. Just as ice skating has become popular because of its beauty, symmetry, and use of music, so musical freestyle is rapidly gaining fans among participants and spectators alike.

A freestyle is a combination of an artistic test you have devised yourself and the music you have selected to accompany it. The USDF has developed their freestyle competition program to encourage riders to be creative and original within the context of classical riding. Many schooling shows allow riders to perform freestyle tests at all the lower levels, although most USDF-rated shows begin to judge them at First Level. If you want to try your hand at developing a musical freestyle, keep in mind that it is more interesting to design your freestyle when there are more movements than Training Level's walking, trotting, and cantering.

The freestyle is judged on technicality and artistic impression. Riders must perform certain compulsory movements according to their riding level within a five-minute time limit. Some of the compulsory movements are performed in both directions. You will only be permitted to perform what is allowed at your particular level, and not above it. When designing your freestyle, pay attention to your horse's gaits, and then select your musical program once you have determined the rhythm and tempo of your horse's three gaits. You can analyze your horse's gaits with a metronome, which can be bought in a music store for about forty dollars. You can get a small, battery-operated metronome that is no larger than a garage door opener. After warming up your horse so that he is limber and moving forward, turn the metronome on and adjust it until you get the same beats per minute as your horse's walk, trot, and canter. (If this is too difficult from the saddle, have a friend adjust the metronome and write down the results.) For the walk, observe your horse's front legs. Do the same for the trot and the canter, except in the canter, you are only tracking one beat (the leading leg).

Next, you need to find music that complements your horse's gaits. Use your metronome, and start listening to all kinds of music. The USDF suggests that you use music that is in the same genre, meaning that you don't want to start off your program with jazz and then move into a Madonna song. It should also have one theme, for instance, all ragtime, all show tunes, or all marching band. As musical freestyles become more popular with spectators, music with vocal tracks will be used more, but they are not as effective as strictly instrumental tracks.

How do you go about searching for the right music? Visit your local libraries and used record stores. Movie soundtracks often have great sweeping scores that can lend themselves to your own freestyle "epic." Swing, big band, and jazz music are also good choices. So are Latin or other instrumentals with exotic rhythms. Look for albums that are compilations, for example, the "best of" a certain musical style or a particular composer, such as Bach, Mozart, or Rossini. Also, choose instrumental artists that have a similar sound from song to song. Pick music that has a simple, distinct beat rather than odd rhythm changes.

Use your metronome to see if the beat of the music you select matches your horse's footfalls. The USDF notes that a strict relationship between music and gaits isn't required, but it does help your overall musical program.

One of the biggest drawbacks that riders have with creating a freestyle tape is that usually a piece of music has one tempo, but the horse has three, so three selections of music are usually made. This often results in poorly edited musical pieces, where the freestyle tape often sounds as though someone has ripped a record player's needle off the record and replaced it with another just as quickly. Some kur music lacks the cohesiveness that is found in an ice skating program.

This is the reason for using film soundtracks or music by the same artist. When editing your five-minute tape, keep in mind that your cuts should be made smoothly and that your segues (going from one piece to the next) should follow logical breaks in the music. Practice fading out the music levels quickly and smoothly, instead of turning off the tape abruptly. Bring up your recording levels in the same manner. Don't be afraid to record several times to get it "just right." That's how you will improve your recording skills and end up with a fine riding tape.

Next, try to make your choreography work with your music. Since you have five minutes, determine which movements are required and which are suggested, and then put together your program according to your horse's best moves. Since you are allowed to use artistic expression, show off what your horse does best and minimize any areas he's weak in. You don't have to stick to the regular places where you execute your movements in your regular tests. You have the whole arena to work in, so use it as an ice skater would. Keep in mind that your test still has to be technically accurate, however.

You should have two copies of your taped music for your freestyle ride, the original and one marked as a backup. This is in case something happens to your original tape (such as warping in the sun or being eaten by the tape player). Both tapes should be cued up and ready to go. Label them with your name, your horse's name, and your riding level. Don't make two separate tapes, as they may differ slightly in editing.

Instead, use a dual-cassette deck to dub the original, or have it professionally duplicated.

Also include an instruction sheet with your name, your horse's name, your bridle number, your ride time and class name and number, and any special instructions about playing your tape.

Freestyles are a great deal of fun to watch, and a well-choreographed one with appropriate music for the horse-and-rider pair is really something special. For full details on how musical freestyles are judged, contact the USDF for their brochure on rules, guidelines, and definitions.

Turning the Sport into Art

Even though you work hard at dressage, you may come across people who are doing better than you because they have a horse that has the ideal movement and aptitude for dressage.

Keep in mind what your own aims are in dressage, and above all, enjoy the time you spend in the sport.

You may encounter a few riders who get high scores in the show ring despite the fact that they don't use classical methods to teach their horses. Try not to get discouraged by either of these scenarios. Quick-fix methods do not get their desired effect for long and indeed have many drawbacks. Keep in mind what your own aims are, and try not to think about what "the other guys" are doing.

Dressage aims to improve the horse and not only develop his body but also his mind. Ideally, by using classical riding, you will have a willing partner. Classical riding is enduring, as it aims for perfection and unity. If you constantly maintain high standards throughout your schooling and in your showing, you can continue to grow in the sport and even take your riding beyond the term *sport*, into art.

Index